BSA Dandy
WORKSHOP MANUAL

A Floyd Clymer Publication
Published in 2022 by VelocePress.com

A Compilation of three factory manuals:
* SERVICE SHEETS *
* ILLUSTRATED PARTS LIST *
* HOW TO RIDE THE BSA DANDY *

© Copyright 2022 Veloce Enterprises Inc. All rights reserved.
This work may not be reproduced or transmitted in any
form without the express written consent of the publisher.

INTRODUCTION

Welcome to the world of digital publishing ~ the book you now hold in your hand was printed using the latest state of the art digital technology. The advent of print-on-demand has forever changed the publishing process, never has information been so accessible and it is our hope that this book serves your informational needs for years to come. If this is your first exposure to digital publishing, we hope that you are pleased with the results. Many more titles of interest to the classic automobile and motorcycle enthusiast, collector and restorer are available via our website at www.VelocePress.com. We hope that you find this title as interesting as we do.

NOTE FROM THE PUBLISHER

The information presented is true and complete to the best of our knowledge. All recommendations are made without any guarantees on the part of the author or the publisher, who also disclaim all liability incurred with the use of this information.

TRADEMARKS

We recognize that some words, model names and designations, for example, mentioned herein are the property of the trademark holder. We use them for identification purposes only. This is not an official publication.

INFORMATION ON THE USE OF THIS PUBLICATION

This manual is an invaluable resource for those interested in performing their own maintenance. However, in today's information age we are constantly subject to changes in common practice, new technology, availability of improved materials and increased awareness of chemical toxicity. As such, it is advised that the user consult with an experienced professional prior to undertaking any procedure described herein. While every care has been taken to ensure correctness of information, it is obviously not possible to guarantee complete freedom from errors or omissions or to accept liability arising from such errors or omissions. Therefore, any individual that uses the information contained within, or elects to perform or participate in do-it-yourself repairs or modifications acknowledges that there is a risk factor involved and that the publisher or its associates cannot be held responsible for personal injury or property damage resulting from the use of the information or the outcome of such procedures.

WARNING!

One final word of advice, this publication is intended to be used as a reference guide, and when in doubt the reader should consult with a qualified technician.

PAGE NUMBERS

Please note that the page numbers relate to the individual manuals. The number to the bottom of the final page is the total number of pages in the manual.

BSA SERVICE SHEETS

BSA 'SERVICE SHEETS'

UNDERSTANDING AND INTERPRETING THE 1945 AND ONWARDS PUBLICATIONS

In 1945, after the war had ended, BSA resumed production of their civilian line of motorcycles. However, they continued their pre-war practice of publishing repair, overhaul and technical information in the form of individual 'Service Sheets'. It should be noted that BSA never intended that these service sheets would be distributed to the general public, they were 'dealer only' publications and, as such, the print quality was at times somewhat questionable. It was not until the early 1960's that BSA eventually started publishing model specific workshop manuals that were available to the general public. Consequently, these 'Service Sheets' were the only publications available for the maintenance and repair of BSA models that were manufactured through the early 1960's.

At some point in the 1930's, BSA adopted the practice of identifying their various model types by 'groups' and the models manufactured from 1945 through the mid 1960's were in Groups A, B, C, D and M. The service sheets that were associated to a particular group were identified numerically and, while there were some exceptions due to overlapping data between models, in general terms the numbers relate to a particular model group. They are as follows: The 200 series of service sheets were applicable to Group A models, the 300 series to Group B, the 400 series to Group C, the 500 series to Group D and the 600 series to Group M. In addition, there were a 700 series applicable to mechanical maintenance and an 800 series for electronic service and wiring diagrams. Both the 700 and 800 series of service sheets contained information that was not model specific but was applicable across multiple model groups. Finally, there were a 900 series for the BSA Dandy and a 1000 series for the BSA Sunbeam and Triumph Tigress scooter.

Unfortunately, as these service sheets were issued individually and at random times, the numbering sequence within any group is, at times, illogical and not necessarily consecutive. Consequently, assembling those individual sheets into a publication that serves as a model specific workshop manual is a somewhat difficult task and owners of BSA motor cycles are subjected to considerable confusion surrounding the appropriate selection from the multitude of reprints that have recently flooded the on-line marketplace. Many of the reprints found on internet websites are from 'bedroom sellers' at enticingly low prices by individuals that really have no idea what they are selling. Many are nothing more than poor quality comb-bound photocopies that are scanned and printed complete with greasy pages and thumbprints and, as such, are deceptively described as 'pre-owned', 'used' or even 'refurbished'! In addition, they are often advertised for the incorrect series and/or model years of motorcycles.

Continued...............

DANDY SERVICE SHEET MANUAL (1957-1962)

The most complete compilation of the 1945 and onwards service sheets was issued by BSA in the form of a 'dealer only' ring binder (See ISBN 9781588502513) that contained all of the individual service sheets totaling to almost 500 pages, it is extremely scarce and difficult to find. This manual includes 8 service sheets (19 pages) published by BSA in the 900 series of service sheets exclusive to the BSA Dandy. However, an additional 6 service sheets (12 pages) have been added from that 'dealer only' publication, to produce a single manual containing all 14 service sheets (31 pages) that cover the 1957 to 1962 Dandy. Please note that service sheets other than those in the 900 series that are included in this publication may also contain data that is applicable to 'other' model groups, as that was the original intention.

INDEX

Page No.	Sheet No.	Description
4	703	Bearing Data
6	704	Piston Data
8	709	Fault Diagnosis
9	710	Chain
11	808K	Wiring Diagrams
13	816	Lucas Alternator
16	901	Engine & Gearbox
17	902	Engine Overhaul
19	903	Engine Removal
23	904	Gearbox Removal
26	905	Gearbox Re-assembly
29	906	Wheels & Brakes
32	907	Frame & Forks
34	908	Technical Data

IMPORTANT NOTE REGARDING MODELS WITH WIPAC ELECTRONICS

Pages 35 to 37 of this manual include 3 wiring diagrams exclusive to Dandy models that were equiped with Wipac electrical systems.

BSA SERVICE SHEET No. 703

Revised Dec. 1958.

All Models

WORKSHOP DATA (BEARINGS) 1956

B.S.A. Part No.	Hoffman No.	Skefko No.	Ransome & Marles No.	British Timkin No.	Fischer No.
24–722	RM.9L	CFM7/C2	MRJA.$\frac{7}{8}$	—	RFM.9
24–724	R.325L	402454.B	MRJA.25	—	MFM.25
24–732	325	6305	MJ.25	—	6305
24–4065	135	6207	LJ.35	—	6207
24–4217	L.S.8	RLS.6	LJ$\frac{3}{4}$	—	LS.8
24–6860	—	2K.1178X 2K.1130N1	—	1178X 1130.N1	—
27–261	MS.9	RM.S7	MJ.$\frac{7}{8}$	—	MS.9
27–4027	LS.11	RL.S9	LJ.$1\frac{1}{8}$	—	—
29–3857	130	6206	LJ.30	—	6206
29–6211	MS.7	RM.S5	MJ.$\frac{5}{8}$	—	MS.7
42–5819	120	—	—	—	—
65–1388	RMS.11	CRM.9	MRJ.$1\frac{1}{8}$	—	RMS.11
65–2045	125	6205	LJ.25	—	6205
65–5883	LS.9	RLS.7	LJ.$\frac{7}{8}$	—	LS.9
67–670	R.130L	NFL.30	LRJA.30	—	NFL.30
89–3022	LS.10	RLS.8	LJ.1	—	LS.10
89–3023	LS.8	RLS.6	LJ.$\frac{3}{4}$	—	LS.8
90–10	117	6203	LJ.17	—	6203
90–11	LS.7	RLS.5	LJ.$\frac{5}{8}$	—	LS.7
90–12	S.9	EE.8J	KLNJ.$\frac{7}{8}$	—	EE.8
90–5525	112	6201	LJ.12	—	6201
90–5559	—	—	—	A.2126	—
90–6063	115	6202	LJ.15	—	6202

B.S.A. SERVICE SHEET No. 703 (continued)

LOCATION OF BEARINGS

Model	Crankcase Roller Bearing Driveside	Crankcase Ball Bearing Driveside	Crankcase Roller Bearing Gearside	Crankcase Ball Bearing Gearside	Crankcase Ball Bearing (Small)	Crankcase Ball Bearing (Large)	Gearbox Pinion Sleeve Ball Bearing	Gearbox Mainshaft Ball Bearing	Front Hub Ball Bearing	Rear Hub Ball Bearing	Rear Hub Brake Drum and C/Wheel Ball Bearing
Dandy	—	—	—	—	90-6063	24-4217	90-6063 (Output shaft)	90-6063 (Input shaft)	—	—	—
D1, D3 & D5	—	—	—	—	90-10	24-4217	90-12	90-11	90-5525	90-6063	—
D1, D3 (Comp.)	—	—	—	—	—	—	—	—	90-5559	—	—
C10L	—	24-732	—	—	—	—	29-3857	90-11	—	90-6063	—
C12	—	24-732	—	—	—	—	29-3857	90-11	65-5383	90-11 O/S 29-6211 N/S	—
C15	—	24-782	—	—	—	—	29-3857	—	90-10	90-10 O/S 42-5819 N/S	—
B31 S/A	24-724	65-2045	24-722	—	—	—	24-4065	24-4217	89-3022	89-3022	89-3022
B31 S/A (1958)	—	—	—	—	—	—	—	—	42-5819	42-5819	89-3022
B32 Comp. Rigid	24-724	65-2045	24-722	—	—	—	24-4065	24-4217	65-5883	65-5883	65-5883
B32/34 Gold Star	65-1338	65-2045	24-722	—	—	—	24-4065	24-4217	65-5883	65-5883	65-5883
B33 S/A	24-724	65-2045	24-722	—	—	—	24-4065	24-4217	89-3022	89-3022	89-3022
B33 S/A (1958)	—	—	—	—	—	—	—	—	42-5819	42-5819	89-3022
B34 Comp. Rigid	24-724	65-2045	24-722	—	—	—	24-4065	24-4217	65-5883	65-5883	65-5883
M21 Rigid	24-724	65-2045	24-722	27-261	—	—	24-4065	24-4217	65-5883	24-6860 (Tapered Roller)	—
M21 Plunger	24-724	65-2045	24-722	27-261	—	—	24-4065	24-4217	65-5883	65-5883	89-3022
M33	24-724	65-2045	24-722	—	—	—	24-4065	24-4217	65-5883	65-5883	89-3022
A7 and Shooting Star	67-670	—	—	—	—	—	24-4065	24-4217	89-3022	89-3022	89-3022
A7 & S/S (1958)	—	—	—	—	—	—	—	—	42-5819	42-5819	89-3022
A10 S/A	67-670	—	—	—	—	—	24-4065	24-4217	89-3022	89-3022	89-3022
A10 S/A (1958)	—	—	—	—	—	—	—	—	42-5819	42-5819	89-3022
A10 Plunger	67-670	—	—	—	—	—	24-4065	24-4217	65-5883	65-5883	89-3022
A10 Road Rocket	67-670	—	—	—	—	—	24-4065	24-4217	65-5883	89-3022	89-3022
A10 Super Rocket	67-670	—	—	—	—	—	24-4065	24-4217	42-5819	42-5819	89-3022

Printed in England   B.S.A. MOTOR CYCLES LTD., Service Dept., Birmingham 11.

BSA SERVICE SHEET No. 704

ALL MODELS
PISTON CLEARANCES

To avoid the possibility of seizure or piston tap, pistons must be fitted with adequate but not excessive clearance.

The following are the recommended total clearances between the bottom of the piston and the cylinder wall.

		MODEL	Tolerances
Dandy 70		7.25 : 1	.003—.004"
D1			.0027—.0045"
D3, C15			.0025—.004"
D5, D7			.003—.005"
C10, C10L			.0045—.0065"
C11, C11G, C12			.0035—.0055"
C15	(Star Group)	6.4 : 1 to 10 : 1	.0017—.0033"
B31			.004—.0055"
B31	(Split skirt)		.0005—.0016"
B32A			.002—.004"
BB32	Gold Star	8 : 1	.003—.0045"
		6.5 : 1	.004—.0055"
		7.5 : 1	.002—.004"
		9 : 1	.003—.0045"
CB32	Gold Star	6.5 : 1	.002—.004"
		8 : 1	.003—.0045"
		8.5 : 1	.003—.0045"
		9 : 1	.003—.0045"
		12.25 : 1	.004—.0055"
		13 : 1	.004—.0055"
DB32	Gold Star	7.25 : 1	.0025—.004"
		8 : 1	.003—.0045"
		9 : 1	.003—.0045"
B40	(Star Group)	7.0 : 1 to 8.7 : 1	.0015—.003"
B33			.0045—.0065"
B33	(Split skirt)		.0006—.00275"
B34A			.0045—.0065"
BB34	Gold Star	7.5 : 1 Standard	.0045—.0065"
		8 : 1	.0025—.0045"
		9 : 1	.0025—.0045"
		6.8 : 1	.0045—.0065"
		11.1	.0025—.0045"
CB34	Gold Star	7.25 : 1	.003—.0045"
		8 : 1	.003—.0045"
		9 : 1	.003—.0045"
DB34	Gold Star	8 : 1	.003—.0045"
DBD34	Gold Star	8.75 : 1	.003—.0045"

B.S.A. Service Sheet No. 704 (contd.)

Model			Tolerances
M20			.004—.006″
M21			.004—.006″
M33			.0045—.0065″
M33	(Split skirt)		.0006—.00275″
A7		6.7 : 1	.002—.004″
	(Split skirt)	6.7 : 1	.0011—.0031″
		7.25 : 1	.002—.004″
	(Split skirt)		.0011—.0031″
A7	(Star Twin)		.002—.004″
A7	(Split skirt)	(Star Twin and Shooting Star)	.001—.0031″
A7	(Shooting Star)	8 : 1 (after Engine No. CA7SS-4501)	.0035—.005″
A50	(Star Twin)	8.0 : 1 to 9.0 : 1	.0011—.0025″
A10	(Golden Flash)	6.5 : 1	.003—.0045″
	(Split skirt)	6.5 : 1	.0025—.0045″
	(Split skirt)	7.25 : 1	.0025—.0045″
A10	(Super Flash and Road Rocket)	8 : 1	.003—.0045″
A10	(Golden Flash)	7.5 : 1 (after Engine No. DA10-651)	.0035—.005″
A10	(Super Rocket)	8.5 : 1 (after Engine No. CA10R-6001)	.004—.0055″
A10	(Rocket Gold Star)	8.75 : 1	.001—.0025″
A65	(Star Twin)	7.5 : 1 to 9.0 : 1	.0012—.0027″

B.S.A. MOTOR CYCLES LTD., Service Department, Armoury Road, Birmingham 11

B.S.A. PRESS

BSA SERVICE SHEET No. 709

ALL MODELS
FAULT FINDING

No adjustments should be made, or any part tampered with, until the cause of the trouble is known. Otherwise adjustments which are correct may be deranged.

Engine Stops Suddenly:
    Petrol shortage in tank, or choked petrol supply pipe or tap.
    Choked main jet, or water in float chamber.
    Oiled up or fouled sparking plug.
    Water on high-tension pick-up or on sparking plug.

Engine Fails to Start, or is difficult to start:
    Lack of fuel, or insufficient flooding if cold.
    Excessive flooding, allowing neat petrol to enter the cylinder.
    Oil sparking plug, or stuck-up valve or valve stem sticky.
    Weak valve spring, or valve not seating properly.
    Throttle opening too large, or pilot jet choked.
    Contact points dirty, or gap incorrect.
    Flat battery, if coil ignition, or faulty electrical connections in ignition circuit.

Loss of Power:
    Valve, or valves, not seating properly.
    Weak valve spring or springs, or sticking valve.
    No tappet clearance, or excessive clearance.
    Lack of oil in tank.
    Brakes adjusted too closely.
    Badly fitting or broken piston rings.
    Punctured carburettor float.
    Incorrect ignition timing.

Engine Overheats:
    Lack of proper lubrication.
    Weak valve springs, or pitted valve seats.
    Worn piston rings, or late ignition setting.
    Carburettor setting too weak, or partly choked petrol pipe.

Engine Misses Fire:
    Weak valve spring.
    Defective or oiled sparking plug, or oil on contact points.
    Incorrectly adjusted contact points or tappets.
    Faulty condenser.
    Defective sparking plug or high-tension cable.
    Loose sparking plug terminal.
    Carburettor flooding, due to stuck or defective float.
    Partly choked main jet.
    Choked vent hole in petrol tank filler cap.

Excessive Oil Consumption:
    Stoppage, or partial stoppage, in pipe returning oil from engine to tank.
    Clogged, or partially clogged, filter in sump, or oil tank.
    Badly worn or stuck-up piston rings, causing high pressure in engine crankcase.
    High crankcase pressure, caused by release valve (breather) action.
    Air leak in dry sump oiling system.
    Non-return valve in system not seating.
    Ball valve in oil pump stuck on its seat.

B.S.A. MOTOR CYCLES LTD., Service Department, Armoury Road, Birmingham 11

B.S.A. PRESS

BSA SERVICE SHEET No. 710

ALL MODELS
CHAIN ALTERATIONS AND REPAIRS

A chain rarely breaks if it is kept properly lubricated and adjusted. Usually it is worn out long before it reaches breaking point. The rear chain is the most heavily stressed and is therefore the one most likely to give trouble. Spare parts should be carried to enable the rider to carry out a repair on the road with the aid of a chain rivet extractor (see Fig. X7). The front chain will probably be worn out before it requires shortening.

How to use the Chain Rivet Extractor
First press down lever (A) Fig. X7 to open the two jaws (B). Insert the link to be removed so that the jaws grip the roller and support the uppermost inner side plate. The punch (C) is then screwed on to the rivet head until the rivet is forced through the outer plate.

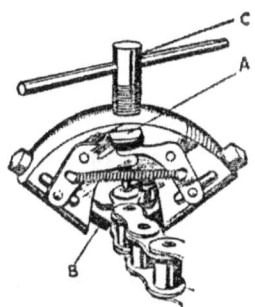

Fig. X7.

To shorten a worn Rear Chain
After a big mileage, the rear chain may have stretched so that no further adjustment is possible by the usual method. In this case it is possible to shorten the chain by one link or pitch, so increasing its useful life. First remove the single connecting spring link (A) securing the two ends of the chain, Fig. X8. If the chain terminates in two ordinary links as in Fig. X8 (in which case the chain will be an even number of pitches) extract the third and fourth rivets (B) from the end and replace the detached three pitches by a single connecting link (C). The connection is made with an additional spring link (D). If one end of the chain has a double cranked link, Fig. X9—in which case the chain will have an odd

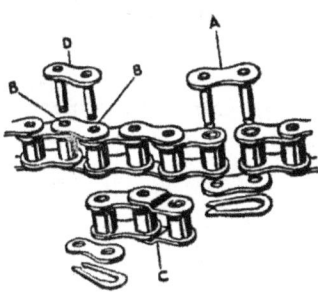

Fig. X8.

Printed in England

B.S.A. Service Sheet No. 710 (contd.)

number of pitches—extract the second and third rivets (A), releasing the cranked link unit complete, which can be retained for further use. Replace with one inner link (B) and again connect up with an additional single connecting link (C).

To repair a damaged Chain

If a roller or link has been damaged (X) Fig. X9, remove rivets (D), take out the damaged link and replace with one inner link, secured by two single connecting links.

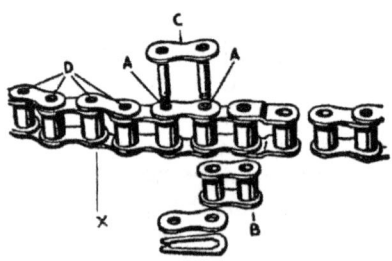

Fig. X9.

It is important that the spring clip fastener should always be put on so that the *closed* end faces the direction of travel of the chain—i.e. when clip is on top run of chain, closed end is toward front of machine—when clip is on bottom run, closed end is towards rear of machine.

It should be noted that once a rivet has been extracted it must not be used again, so that it is important to check that the correct rivet is being removed before actually removing it. In the case of double cranked links, the complete unit comprises an inner link and the cranked outer link—three rollers in all—and these must never be separated.

Fitting Rear Chain

To fit a new rear chain, turn wheel until the spring link of the old chain is located on rear sprocket. Disconnect, and allow the lower run to drop down. Join the top run of the old chain to the new chain by means of the connecting link, and then by pulling on the bottom run of the old chain the new one will be carried round the gearbox sprocket. Then the old chain can be disconnected and the ends of the new one joined together.

When the rear chain breaks and falls from its sprockets, the new or repaired chain can be replaced without taking off the chainguards. One end of the chain must be fed (from the rear) under the front end of the rear top chainguard on to the gearbox sprocket A long bladed screwdriver or a piece of stiff wire may assist this operation When the chain has located on the sprocket teeth, engage a gear and gently turn gearbox over with the kickstarter This will feed chain round gearbox sprocket When sufficient length of chain is hanging below sprocket, disengage gear and chain can then be pulled round until both runs can be fed inside rear chainguard and engaged on rear wheel sprocket.

B.S.A. MOTOR CYCLES LTD., Service Department, Armoury Road, Birmingham 11.

BSA SERVICE SHEET No. 808K

Printed March, 1959

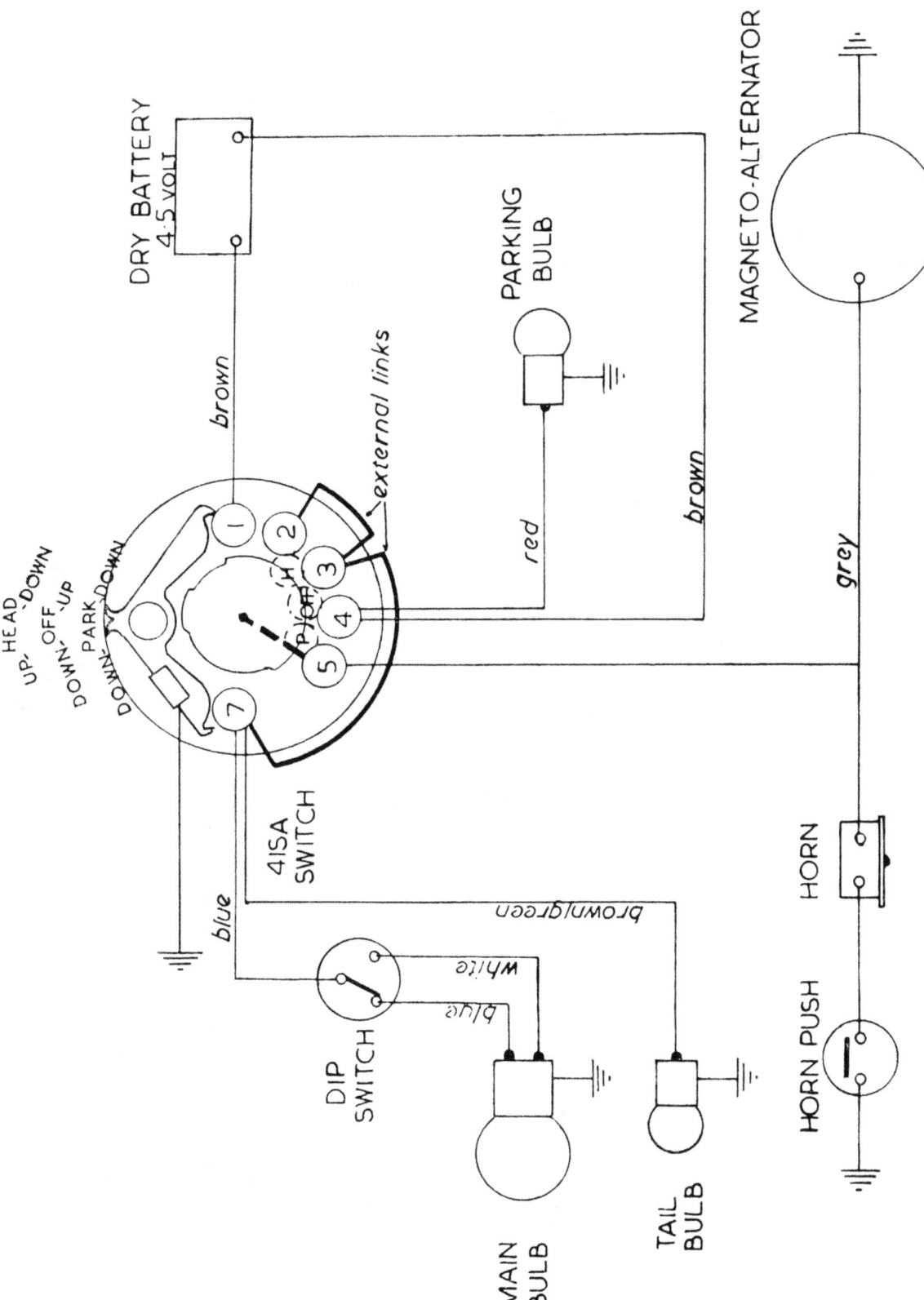

B.S.A. "DANDY 70"—WIRING CIRCUIT
WITH 41SA LIGHTING SWITCH (SEPARATE DIPPER SWITCH)

B.S.A. Service Sheet No. 808K (contd.)

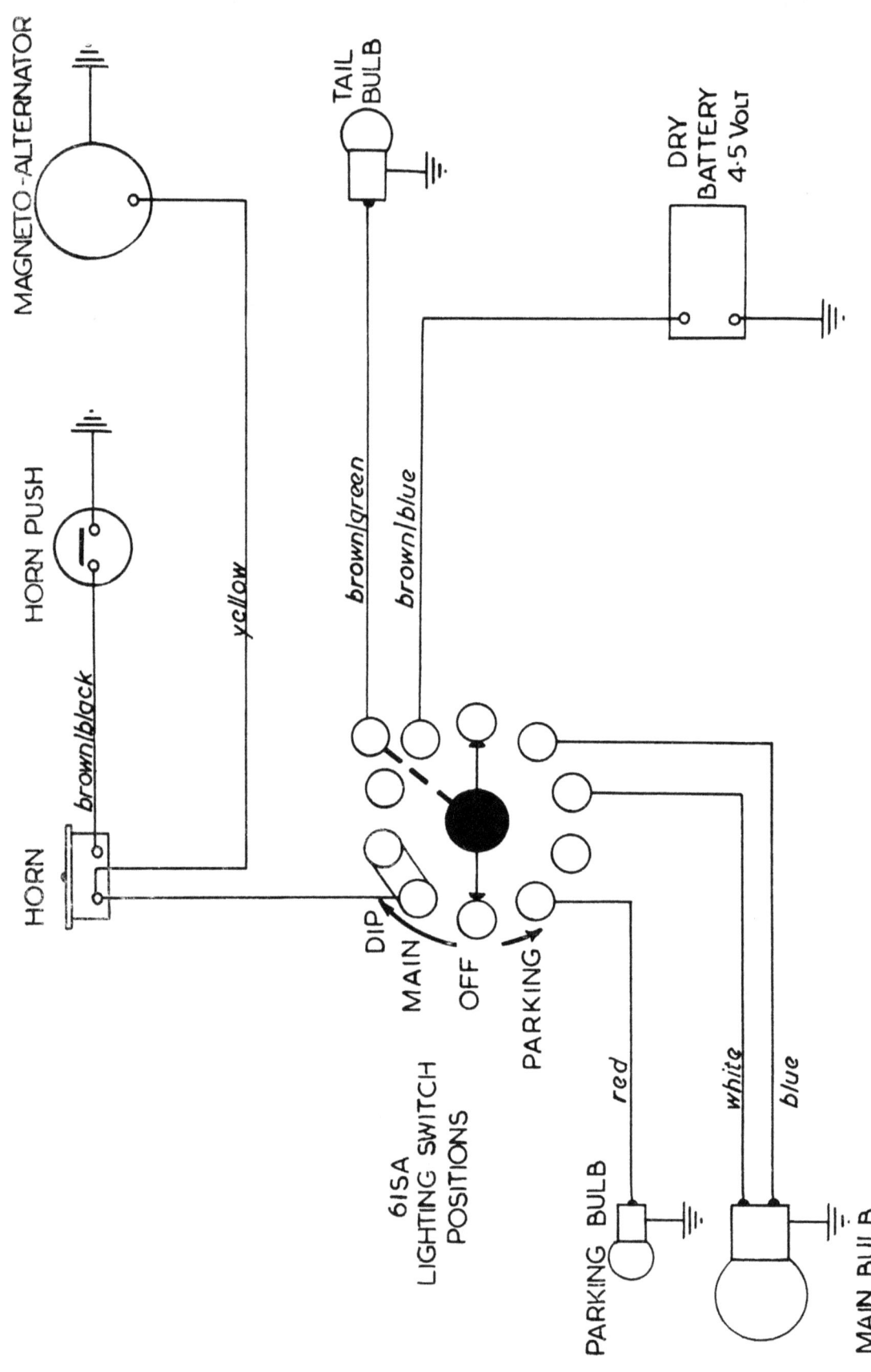

B.S.A. "DANDY 70"—WIRING CIRCUIT
WITH 61SA LIGHTING SWITCH, INCORPORATING DIP POSITION

B.S.A. MOTOR CYCLES LTD., Service Dept., Waverley Works, Birmingham 10.

Printed in England.

BSA SERVICE SHEET No. 816

October 1964

DANDY 70
LUCAS ELECTRICAL EQUIPMENT
(Fitted on and after Engine No. DSE14103
(FLYWHEEL MAGNETO-ALTERNATOR MODEL 8FI)

The flywheel magneto-alternator model 8FI employs conventional ignition and lighting circuits, and therefore differs from model 6FI previously fitted to these machines. Maintenance and servicing are quite straight forward and will be helped by the following information:—

MAINTENANCE.

Every 5,000 miles or when the engine is removed for decarbonisation, check and clean the contact breaker.

The felt lubricating pad should be renewed or re-lubricated with clean engine oil (S.A.E. 40/50) every 5,000 miles. Also lightly oil the contact lever pivot.

Should it be necessary to renew the contact breaker, the toothed retaining ring which secures the lever to the pivot post must be prised off and a new ring fitted on re-assembly. The pivot post should first be smeared with Mobilgrease No. 2.

DATA.

Main bulb: Lucas 387 6 volt 18/18 watt (non-reversible).
Parking bulb: Lucas No. 974, 3.5 volt 0.15 amp.
Rear lamp bulb: Lucas No. 990, 6 volt 3 watt.
Ignition timing: 5/32 in. B.T.D.C.
Contact breaker gap: .014 — .016 in.

FAULT LOCATION.
Equipment Required:

(a) A good quality rectified moving coil voltmeter, scale 0—10 volts, with divisions enabling accurate readings of 0.2-volt to be made.
(b) A 1.2 ohm load resistor, non-inductively wound and capable of carrying 5-amp. without exceeding 5% variation in resistance at that current.
(c) A stationary three-point spark gap (as used for coil ignition testing) set to 4 mm. Alternatively, an approved two-point adjustable spark gap set to 4 mm. can be used for ignition tests carried out with the unit in situ on the engine.
(d) Fully charged 6-volt battery.
(e) Moving coil ammeter, scale 0—20 amp.

Note.—Under no circumstances must moving iron meters be used, or a D.C. current allowed to flow through the alternator with the rotor fitted.

TESTING.
1. **Engine fails to start:**
    (i) Set lighting switch to OFF.
    (ii) Disconnect H.T. lead at sparking plug and connect 4 mm. spark gap between H.T. lead and earth (i.e., frame of engine block). The gap should spark at normal "foot-start" speed. If it does, remove sparking plug, clean and reset. Also check fuel supply etc., and do not forget that ignition timing is a critical factor in starting.

B.S.A. Service Sheet No. 816 (contd.)

- (iii) If there is no spark, or if engine still cannot be started, check ignition system as follows:—
  - (a) Remove engine from frame.
  - (b) Check that contact breaker gap is correctly set.
  - (c) Remove flywheel using B.S.A. Extractor Tool No. 61-3540.
  - (d) Connect 4 mm. spark gap between end of H.T. lead and earth on stator.
  - (e) Connect positive terminal of 6-volt battery to stator earth nearest to ignition coil, using a jumper lead.
  - (f) Hold contact breaker open by means of a piece of thick card between contacts, then connect one end of a second jumper lead to moving contact arm (take care not to short it to stationary contact which is earthed).
  - (g) With free end of second jumper lead, quickly make and break circuit to battery negative terminal. (Make this test as short as possible to avoid overheating ignition coil primary winding). A spark should be obtained at two-point gap.
- (iv) If only a weak spark, or no spark, is obtained, substitute a new condenser and retest. Since the condenser relies on its electrical connection with clip, outside case should be cleaned with a petrol-moistened cloth. Solvents must not be used for this purpose.
- (v) If trouble persists, check coil. To do this, connect a 2-volt cell of battery between primary coil earth connection on stator, and primary coil connection at condenser or on the moving contact arm, with ammeter (item *e*) in series, and contacts remaining separated by the card. Since resistance of primary winding is approximately 1 ohm, a reading of 2 amp. should be given if coil is in order. If reading is zero or low, and cause is not due to faulty external connections at earth point or condenser, an indication is given of an open circuit in coil. A reading in excess of 2 amp. indicates short-circuited primary turns and in either event, a replacement stator will be necessary.
- (vi) After any renewal of parts, adjust contact gap and refit flywheel, using B.S.A. Service Tool No. 61-3536. Check by spinning engine over by hand with H.T. lead connected to sparking plug which has been unscrewed and placed on engine block. If possible, bench test magneto-alternator before refitting engine (see para. 5).

2. **Engine difficult to start, or runs intermittently:**
   If after checking as detailed in (i) to (iii), trouble persists it will be necessary to proceed as laid down in (iv) to (vi).

3. **No Lights with Lighting Switch in Head or Dip Position and Engine Running.**
   - (vii) Disconnect alternator main lead from wiring harness, and to it connect one side of voltmeter and also one side of 1.2-ohm load resistor. Connect other voltmeter lead, and that of resistor, to engine block. Voltmeter and resistor are now in parallel across lighting coils.
   - (viii) Start engine and increase speed slowly. Voltmeter should indicate rising volts with speed, increasing to between 3.5 and 7.5 volts.
   - (ix) If satisfactory, check headlamp and rear lamp bulbs, by substitution if necessary. Check wiring and connections between headlamp and switch, rear lamp and switch, and alternator and switch, rectifying as necessary. Fit new lighting switch if necessary.

Note.—Poor earth connections can be particularly troublesome, and will cause high voltages which reduce bulb life. Burnt-out or blackened bulbs often indicate the existence of bad earths, which should be rectified before fitting new bulbs.

B.S.A. Service Sheet No. 816 (contd.)

(x) If rising voltage characteristic is not obtained see (viii), alternator will have to be removed from the machine and flywheel taken off. Using one 2-volt cell of test battery, connect positive battery terminal to earth on engine, negative battery terminal to one ammeter terminal, and second ammeter terminal to main output lead of alternator. Reading obtained on ammeter should be approximately 9.5 amp. (lighting coils are connected in parallel with a joint resistance of about 0.2 ohm). **DO NOT ALLOW THIS CURRENT TO FLOW FOR MORE THAN ONE SECOND.**

(xi) A higher reading, in region of 15—20 amp., will indicate short-circuited windings on one or both coils. A reading in the order of 5 amp. will indicate an open circuit in one of the coils and in either event, a replacement stator will be necessary. Zero reading indicates an open circuit, possibly in alternator lead, while a reading lower than 9.5 but exceeding 5 indicates faulty continuity. Check leads and coil earthing points.

Note.—This test must be done as quickly as possible to avoid damage to coils through over-heating, and misleading readings due to increase in coil resistance with temperature. It will be found that one second's duration gives ample time to observe the ammeter readings. **On no account must test be made with alternator assembled to a bench testing jig with flywheel fitted, otherwise partial de-magnetisation will result.**

(xii) After renewal of any necessary parts, refit flywheel. If possible, bench test alternator before refitting engine (see para. 4).

4. **BENCH TESTING.**

   (a) **Ignition Performance.**

   This test is made with H.T. lead connected to a stationary three-point spark gap set to 4 mm. Regular sparking should occur at all speeds above 1,000 r.p.m.

   (b) **Alternator Output Performance on Load.**

   Connect one voltmeter lead to alternator main output lead, and second voltmeter lead to stator. Similarly, connect 1.2-ohm load resistor across alternator between main output lead and stator. Run up alternator speed and check output voltages as follows:—

R.P.M.		Voltmeter Reading.
2,000	not **less** than	3.7
4,000	not **less** than	5.4
6,000	not **less** than	6.0
8,000	not **more** than	7.25

B.S.A. MOTOR CYCLES LTD.,
Service Dept., Armoury Road, Birmingham 11
B.S.A. Press.

BSA SERVICE SHEET No. 901

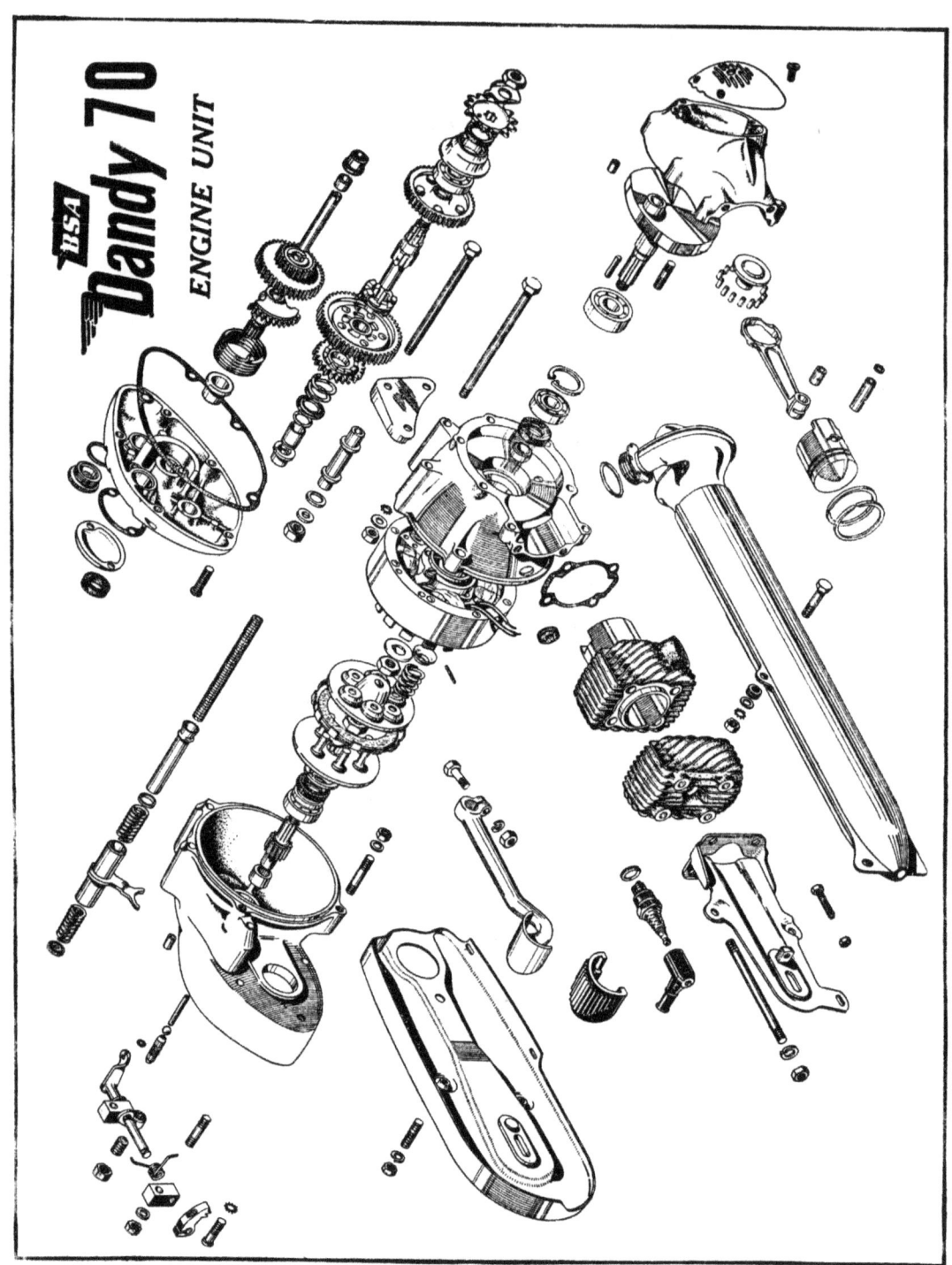

The DANDY Engine and Gearbox (Exploded View)

BSA SERVICE SHEET No. 902

Dandy 70

DECARBONISATION

To maintain the engine in an efficient condition, it is recommended that decarbonising should be carried out at intervals of approximately 1,500 miles. A two-stroke engine is particularly affected by the formation of carbon. The symptoms indicating an excessive deposit are rough and uneven running of the engine, a tendency to pink when under load, a falling off in power and four or eight stroking when running lightly loaded.

Not only the cylinder head and piston crown will require clearing of carbon, but also the exhaust port and silencing system.

To remove the cylinder head and barrel, first take off the right-hand wheel spindle nut "A," Fig. Z1, and partly withdraw the spindle towards the left-hand side. Unscrew the small nut and bolt "B," holding the silencer to the swinging arm plate, and release the silencer from the cylinder barrel by unscrewing the union nut "C," using the special spanner provided in the tool-kit.

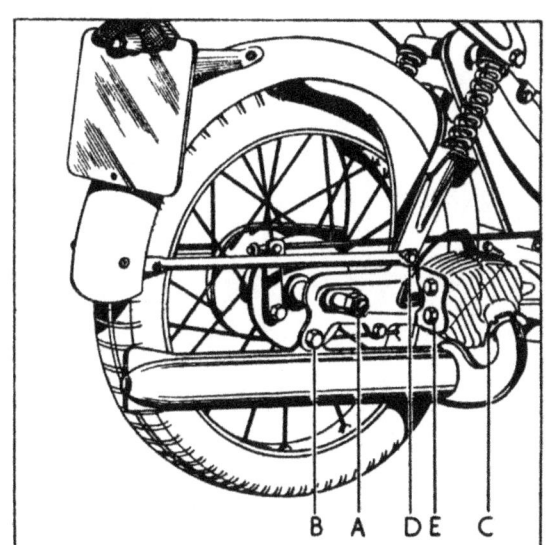

Fig. Z1. Removal of Cylinder Head and Barrel.

Next remove the two bolts "D," which secure the swinging arm plate to the rear fork, noting the positions of the distance piece, the fork end stiffening plate, and the brake anchor strap. Unscrew the sparking plug and take off the four cylinder head nuts "E." The swinging arm plate and cylinder head can now be drawn away from the barrel. It is best to clear the carbon from the piston crown at this stage, taking care not to score the soft aluminium.

The cylinder barrel itself has a long spigot fitting into the crankcase, which has two studs at this point, one above and one below the spigot. The nuts on these studs must be slackened before the cylinder barrel can be withdrawn. As the piston emerges from the cylinder, it must be supported to avoid damage. Inspect the piston rings to see that they are quite free in their grooves. Clean out the various ports in the cylinder, but be careful not to remove any metal by over-enthusiastic scraping.

Wipe all traces of loose carbon from the piston and cylinder bore, apply a little clean oil and re-fit the cylinder, making sure that the piston rings are properly seated with their ends resting either side of the pegs in the grooves. A new cylinder base washer should be used.

B.S.A. Service Sheet No. 902—*continued*

Carefully scrape the carbon from the combustion space in the cylinder head, and replace the head on the barrel so that the finning matches up. Follow on with the remaining parts in reverse order to that in which they were removed, not forgetting to tighten the two nuts at the base of the cylinder after the four cylinder head nuts have been tightened fully.

As the silencer is non-detachable, it must be soaked in a caustic soda solution, preferably overnight, and then thoroughly washed out in running water. On no account should the caustic solution be allowed to touch any of the aluminium or painted parts of the machine.

B.S.A. MOTOR CYCLE LTD.,
Service Department, Armoury Road,
Birmingham, II.
Printed in England.

BSA SERVICE SHEET No. 903

June 1957
Reprinted November 1962

Dandy 70

REMOVAL OF ENGINE FROM FRAME, DISMANTLING AND RE-ASSEMBLING

Take off the carburetter cover plate "B," Fig. Z2, which is retained by three screws, and pull the carburetter away from the crankcase leaving the cable and petrol pipe attached. Tie the instrument up out of harms way.

Remove the right-hand wheel spindle nut and the two bolts holding the swinging arm blade to the rear fork (see Fig. Z1, Service Sheet No. 902). Partly withdraw the wheel spindle towards the left-hand side.

Disconnect the lead from the generator at the snap connector which will be found inside the frame behind the large rubber cover. Pull the lead clear of the frame.

Unscrew the six nuts "A," Fig. Z2. Take off the engine plate. The engine can now be drawn away complete with the silencer and the swinging arm blade.

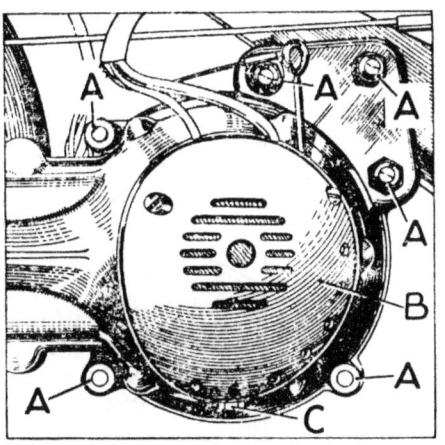

Fig. Z2. Removing Engine.

CONTACT POINTS—WICO GENERATOR

If the purpose in removing the engine is to clean or adjust the contact-breaker points "B," Fig. Z3, the flywheel must be drawn off. Bend back the locking washer and unscrew the nut, holding the flywheel by inserting Service Tool No. 61-3551 through the two holes in the sides of the clutch driving cup. A suitable tommy bar or long bolt placed in one of the crankcase lugs will prevent rotation.

The mainshaft is a parallel fit in the flywheel, which is keyed in position. To withdraw the flywheel use Service Tool No. 61-3540, or a pair of No. 61-3548 in conjuction with an Extractor No. 61-3256.

Turn the engine until the points are fully open and adjust the gap to .018"—.020" by slackening the fixing screw "D" and turning the eccentric adjusting screw "E." Re-tighten the fixing screw.

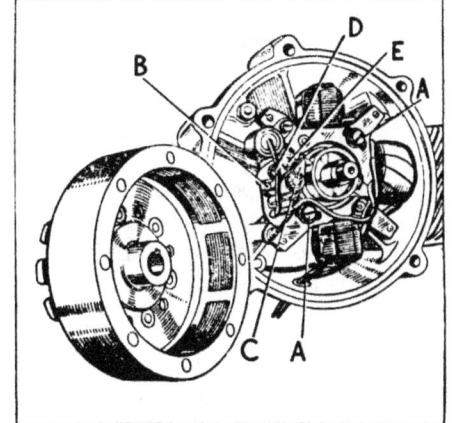

Fig. Z3. Generator (Wico)

B.S.A. Service Sheet No. 903—*continued*

To remove the points assembly; take out the fixing screw and detach the two wires which are secured by a small screw and nut. The points can be cleaned by lightly polishing with smooth emery cloth. Lubricate the felt pad by working into it a small quantity of motor transmission grease. Do not use ordinary grease.

CONTACT POINTS—LUCAS GENERATOR

Models having a Lucas generator can be identified by the letter "L" included in the engine number prefix.

In this case it is not necessary to withdraw the flywheel to check and adjust the points. An opening is provided in the face of the flywheel for this purpose.

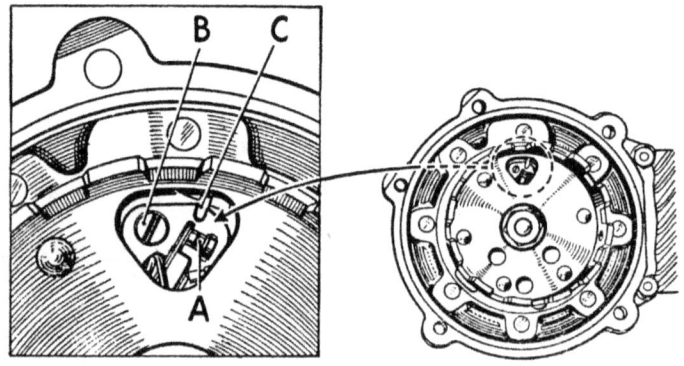

Fig. Z4. Adjusting the Contact Breaker Points (Lucas).

Rotate the flywheel until the opening is in line with the contact-breaker and the points are fully open. Slacken the fixing screw "B," Fig. Z4, place the end of the screwdriver in the slot "C" and move the plate as necessary to obtain the correct points gap of .014″—.016″. Re-tighten the fixing screw.

To remove the points assembly, the flywheel must be drawn off as already described. Take out the fixing screw and remove the nut from the terminal post, noting the positions of the various washers. Carefully prise off the return spring and lift off the two wires. The points assembly can then be removed. Very fine emery cloth may be used to clean the points.

The felt pad should be removed or re-impregnated with clean engine oil. Lubricate the contact lever pivot with a spot of engine oil.

Note.—Before re-fitting the flywheel, make sure that no metallic particles have been attracted on to the magneto. Always use Service Tool No. 61-3536 to avoid placing any strain on the con-rod assembly. Fit a new locking washer under the nut.

B.S.A. Service Sheet No. 903—*continued*

TO CHECK IGNITION TIMING

Remove the sparking plug and turn the engine in an anti-clockwise direction (looking at the generator side) until the piston is at the top of its stroke. Then turn back until the piston has moved 5/32in. from T.D.C. In this position the cam on the mainshaft should be just commencing to lift the contact-breaker rocker arm "C," Fig. Z3 or "B," Fig. Z5, and the points should be not more than .002in. apart. If they are open more than this, the timing is too far advanced. If they are open less, the timing is retarded.

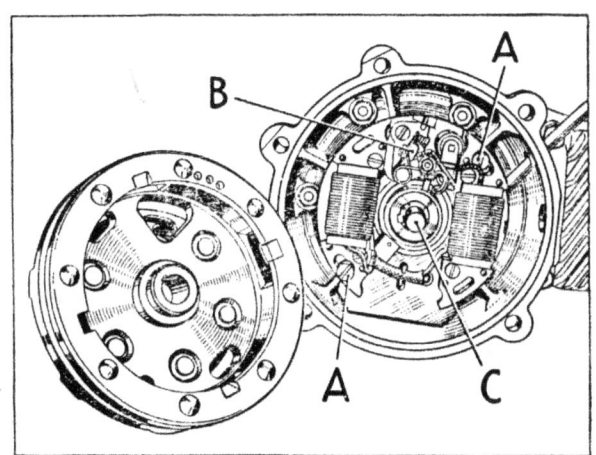

Fig. Z5. Generator (Lucas).

The cam itself is keyed to the mainshaft, but a small adjustment can be made to the timing by slackening the two screws "A," Figs. Z3 or Z5, and moving the stator assembly either way as necessary. After re-timing, tighten the screws firmly.

COMPLETE DISMANTLING OF THE ENGINE

Take out the two screws "A," Figs. Z3 or Z5, and withdraw the stator assembly, pulling the two leads through the rubber grommet in the housing. Prise off the contact-breaker cam and lever the key out of the shaft with a small screwdriver or similar tool.

Remove the swinging arm blade, cylinder head and cylinder barrel as described in Service Sheet No. 902. The gudgeon pin is secured in the piston by means of circlips. Take out one of these with a pair of thin-nosed pliers, warm the piston by applying a cloth soaked in hot water and press out the gudgeon pin. Support the piston firmly during this operation to avoid straining the con-rod.

Now unscrew the five crankcase stud nuts from inside the generator housing, and also the two nuts at the base of the cylinder. The outer crankcase half can then be drawn away. As the crankpin is of the overhung type, both main bearings are contained in the inner half of the crankcase. Press the mainshaft assembly out of these bearings. Note that the crankpin is not detachable; should it be necessary to renew the big-end bearing, a complete new mainshaft assembly must be used.

An oil seal is located behind the contact-breaker cam. This can be prised out of the housing after the small ring has been removed from its centre. Both main bearings must be extracted from the right-hand side of the housing by means of a suitable drift or puller. The smaller bearing is retained by a spring ring. Heat the crankcase in hot water before attempting to remove or replace the bearings.

RE-ASSEMBLING THE ENGINE

Re-assembly is carried out in the reverse order to dismantling; using a new oil seal on the engine mainshaft.

B.S.A. Service Sheet No. 903—*continued*

Inspect the piston and rings; discoloured patches on the outer surfaces of the rings indicate a leakage of gas from the combustion chamber and the rings should be renewed.

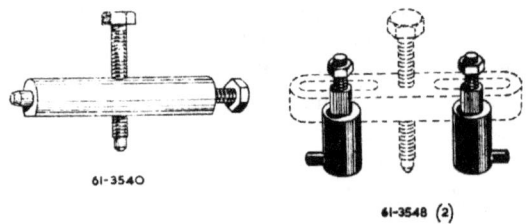

The skirt of the piston should present a dull, even surface. High spots will show up as small bright patches, and these may be very slightly eased with a very fine file. Heavy scores denote a partial seizure, possibly caused by insufficient lubrication, a too weak fuel mixture or retarded ignition, any of which would result in overheating. Fit a new piston after the cause of the trouble has been investigated and cured. Check that the rings are a close fit in the grooves; there should be no noticeable side play. The ring gaps should be not more than .013in., or less than .009in. To measure the gaps accurately, place each ring squarely in the cylinder bore, preferably near the base where the least wear takes place.

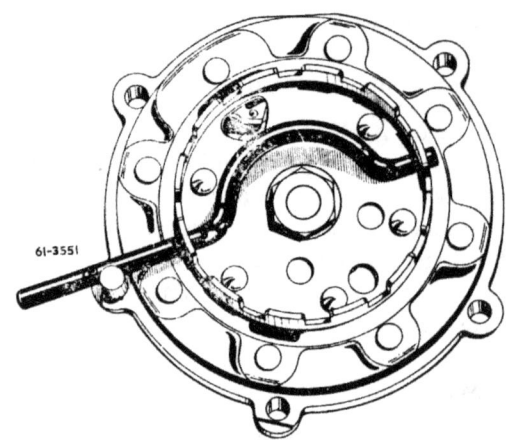

The crown of the piston is marked "EXHAUST" on one side. This side must be next to the exhaust port in the cylinder; that is, on the right-hand side of the engine. Failure to observe

Fig. Z6. Flywheel Removal Tools.

this precaution may result in the ends of the rings becoming trapped in the cylinder ports.

Do not forget to adjust the contact points gap before replacing the flywheel on a Wico generator.

A useful tool for turning up the locking washer on to the flywheel nut consists of a substantial flat bar which has the end bent at right-angles and ground to a wedge shape. Rest the wedge behind the washer and strike the flat of the bar with a hammer.

When the re-assembly is completed, replace the engine in the frame and securely tighten all nuts and screws. It will be noticed that the carburetter is a push fit into a plastic sleeve in the crankcase. Two rubber rings in grooves on the carburetter spigot provide a seal. These may require renewing occasionally to ensure an air-tight joint.

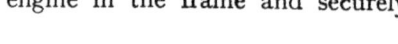

Fig. Z7. Flywheel Assembly Tool.

B.S.A. MOTOR CYCLES LTD.,
Service Department,
Armoury Road,
Birmingham, 11.
Printed in England

BSA SERVICE SHEET No. 904

June 1957
Reprinted November 1962.

Dandy 70

REMOVAL OF GEARBOX FROM FRAME, AND DISMANTLING

First, take out the rear wheel, as described in Service Sheet No. 906. Release the clutch and preselector cables from the handlebar controls. The clutch cable nipple is mounted in a slotted adaptor in the control lever, and can be slipped out once the outer cable is detached from the control body.

Pull off the plastic grip from the preselector control; if this proves to be a tight fit it can be eased by applying a cloth soaked in hot water. Screw in the adjuster at the rear of the gearbox until sufficient slack cable has been obtained to enable the retainer "A," Fig. Z8, to be removed from the end of the twistgrip. The cable adjuster is locked by means of a plate secured to an adjacent stud or, on early models, by a locknut.

Inside the handlebar will be found the cable stop positioning rod "B," which also serves to lock the guide screw "D." Unscrew the rod several turns and take out the guide screw. The cable stop "C" can then be pulled out by means of the rod, and the cable withdrawn from the handlebar. Before drawing the two cables down through the frame, tie a length of stout string to each so that it can be used to assist in threading the cables back again.

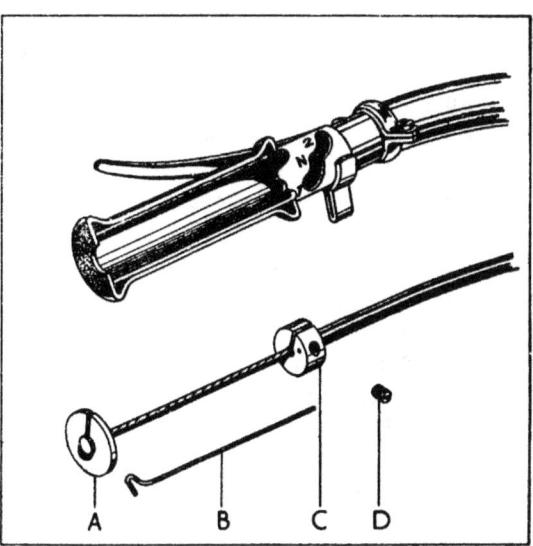

Fig. Z8. Preselector Control Assembly.

An alternative is to detach the cables from the gearbox end, and this is the best method if the intention is to dismantle the gearbox. To do this, the gearbox cover must be removed by unscrewing the five screws around the outer edge, not forgetting to place a tray underneath to catch the oil.

Select second gear and operate the clutch lever, then turn the control to the first gear position but do not touch the clutch lever again. Screw in the cable adjuster until the cable is slack enough to allow the anchor plate to be removed from the outer end of the gear shifter. The adjuster can then be completely unscrewed and the cable pulled out of the gearbox.

B.S.A. Service Sheet No. 904—continued

Next, the clutch adjuster should be screwed down, and the push-rod adjusting screw slackened right off; so that by lifting the withdrawal lever, the cable nipple may be disengaged. Note that, as soon as the clutch withdrawal lever is lifted, the gear shifter will spring outwards and may push the first gear pinion off its shaft if not held in place. If difficulty is experienced in disengaging the cable nipple due to lack of clearance behind the lever, the two nuts holding the locking arm spindle may be loosened a few turns and the whole assembly moved outwards a small amount. When the cable is free, unscrew the adjuster and take away the cable. Replace the gearbox cover temporarily to prevent the ingress of dirt and to keep the internal parts in place.

Remove the two bolts "A," Fig. Z9, from the rear fork end, and also the bolt "B," which passes through the chaincase into the mudguard valance. There are no loose distance pieces or nuts on the bolts, but there is a distance piece fixed to the mudguard valance, and the chain and chaincase must be guided clear of this as the gearbox is taken away. Unscrew the six nuts "A." (See Fig. Z2, Service Sheet No. 903.)

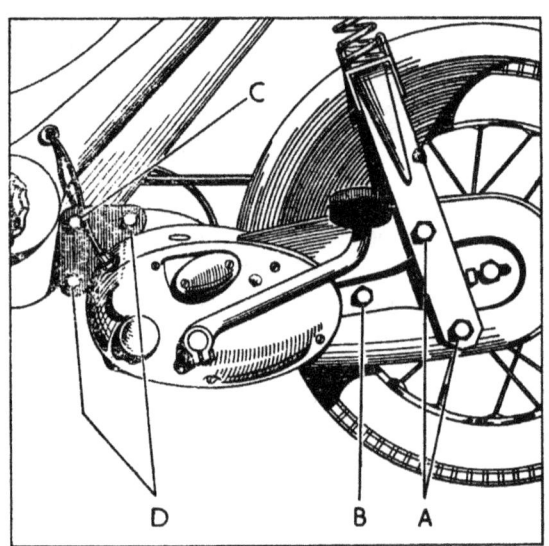

Fig. Z9 Removal of Gearbox.

Pull out the three bolts, and replace them from the opposite side to support the engine. The gearbox complete with chaincase can now be removed.

Should it be desired to remove the engine and gearbox as a unit, carry out the operations described in this Sheet and those in Service Sheet No. 903. Only the two engine plate bolts "D" Fig. Z9 need to be taken out, the pivot bolt and engine plates being left in position on the frame.

DISMANTLING THE GEARBOX

Drain out the oil, if this has not already been done. Slacken the pinch bolt in the starting lever and pull the lever off the splines on the quadrant spindle. Remove the cover and withdraw the quadrant, first noting the location of the return spring. The bush may be pressed out towards the inside of the cover, after the felt oil seal and retaining collar have been prised out.

The first gear pinion and the ratchet pinion are held together by means of a spring, collar and circlip. They can be lifted off the output shaft as a unit and need not be separated unless one of the components is to be renewed. Next, the sliding dog and the gear shifter should be taken out, followed by the locking arm spindle assembly after removal of the two nuts.

B.S.A. Service Sheet No. 904—*continued*

The clutch is dismantled quite simply by compressing the springs by hand, one by one, and removing the cotter pins "B," Fig. Z10, the collars "A" and the springs. This releases the pressure plate and the driving plate, leaving the back plate secured by a central nut. Bend back the lock-washer and place Service Tool No. 61-3553 over the six pins in the back plate, with the holes in the arms located over two of the housing studs. Unscrew the nut and lift off the back plate.

It is not advisable to use an ordinary sprocket puller to remove the back plate, owing to the risk of distortion. If the plate is a tight fit on the splines, a sharp tap with a mallet on the end of the shaft will free it.

Behind the back plate will be seen the end of the gear cluster spindle, which is slotted and pinned to prevent rotation. Tap this spindle out, using a suitable drift, and remove the gear cluster.

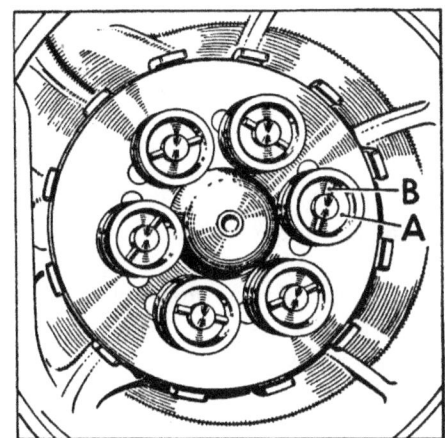

Fig. Z10. Clutch Springs.

Unscrew the sprocket securing nut after bending back the lock-washer, holding the sprocket with Service Tool No. 61-3554. Take off the sprocket and press the shaft through towards the inside of the gearbox. The second gear pinion can now be removed. The bearing and oil seal are housed in a steel sleeve in the gearbox casing. Prise out the oil seal and press out the bearing, again towards the inside of the gearbox.

Extract the clutch push rod from the input shaft. This is in two parts with a ball bearing between, the shorter portion having a rubber oil seal ring fitted in a groove. Remove the circlip from the clutch side of the housing and press the shaft out in that direction complete with the bearing, oil seal and oil seal ring. The needle roller bearing, which supports the other end of the shaft, can be pressed out either way.

B.S.A. MOTOR CYCLES LTD.,
Service Department, Armoury Road,
Birmingham, 11.
Printed in England

BSA SERVICE SHEET No. 905

June 1957
Reprinted November 1962

Dandy 70

RE-ASSEMBLING THE GEARBOX

Fit the needle roller bearing into its housing and insert the input shaft, place the ballrace over the shaft and press into position. Follow on with the oil seal ring and oil seal, and replace the circlip, then replace the clutch backplate and secure it with the nut and lockwasher. Service Tool No. 61-3553 will hold the backplate while the nut is tightened.

Press the output shaft ballrace into the steel sleeve, pass the shaft through the second gear pinion and into the bearing, making sure that the side of the pinion with which the sliding dog engages is facing outwards.

Place the gear cluster into position, line up the slot in the end of the spindle with the pin in the housing and press it home. To guard against oil leakage, the end of the spindle should be coated with jointing compound.

Next, fit the oil seal, sprocket, lockwasher and nut to the output shaft. Tighten the nut while holding the sprocket with Service Tool No. 61-3554. Always use new lockwashers and turn them up securely against the nuts after tightening. New oil seals should also be fitted when re-assembling.

Complete the clutch assembly by fitting the driving and pressure plates, and the springs, collars and cotter pins. It is preferable to use new springs if the originals have already seen a period of service.

At this stage, the gearbox can be re-fitted to the machine, not forgetting to place the driving chain around the sprocket, with the closed end of the connecting link spring facing forward on the top run. Replace the bolts and nuts shown in Figs. Z2 and Z9, (see Service Sheets Nos. 903 and 904).

Assemble the gear shifter, noting the correct positions of the springs, shown in Fig. Z11. The cranked portion of the fork faces outwards, so that the projection with which the locking arm engages is to the front of the gearbox. Place the sliding dog in the shifter fork and fit the assembly into the gearbox. The sliding dog must engage the splines on the out-put shaft and the shifter tube enter into its housing. Pass the cable through and screw in the adjuster until the anchor plate can be replaced behind the nipple. To obtain the maximum amount of slack cable, the handlebar control should be in the first gear position and the gear shifter pushed right home so that the sliding dog engages second gear.

B.S.A. Service Sheet No. 905—*continued*

The shifter tube on early models was without the washer brazed to the inner end which serves to centralise the tube. To fit the modified part, it may, in some cases, be necessary to ream out the housing in the gearbox shell to its full depth, using a standard 13/16in. reamer. With the modified shifter tube, later type springs should also be fitted. These are longer than the originals and are identified by a yellow paint marking.

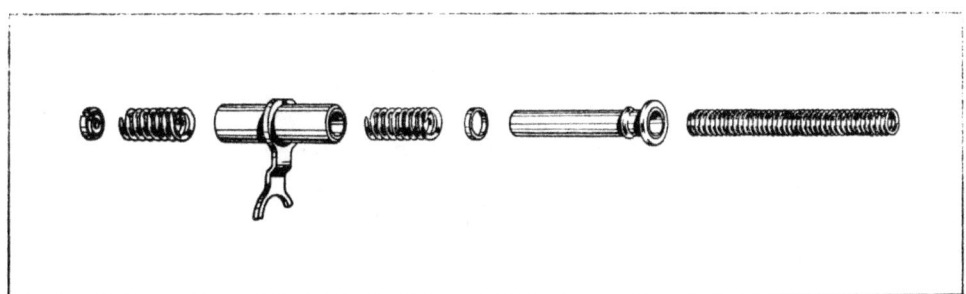

Fig. Z11. Gear Shifter Fork Assembly.

Lightly grease the long clutch pushrod and the ball bearing, and insert them into the hollow input shaft, followed by the short pushrod. The latter has an "O" ring in the middle groove to act as an oil seal; see that this is intact. Take the locking arm spindle assembly and connect the clutch cable to the withdrawal lever. At the same time, fit the two alloy bearing blocks over their studs and start the nuts. One end of the return spring should be located in a hole in the side of the clutch operating arm, while the other end bears on the underside of the top of the gearbox casing. Check that the pushrod adjusting screw is slackened off, and that the locking arm is not fouling the gear shifter. Tighten up the two nuts.

Make sure that the clutch withdrawal lever is at the bottom of its travel. If necessary, slacken the pinch screw "D," Fig. Z12, in the locking arm at the other end of the spindle to prevent the arm being held up by the gear shifter. Screw out the cable adjuster "C," until there is approximately ⅛in. free play in the cable. Turn the pushrod adjuster "B" in a clockwise direction until resistance is felt; then back off half a turn and tighten the locknut "A."

Replace the first gear assembly on the output shaft. Fit the starter quadrant and spring to the cover and re-fit the cover to the gearbox, using a new gasket and a smear of jointing compound to ensure an oil-tight joint. On early models there will sometimes be a shim inside the hollow quadrant spindle to limit the clearance at the end of the gear cluster spindle. The depth of the spigot hole in the quadrant must be approximately .010in. greater than the length of spindle protruding from the gear cluster. If the clearance at this point is too large, it is possible for the spindle to move outwards until an oil leak occurs past the slotted end.

B.S.A. Service Sheet No. 905—*continued*

Set the pre-selector control to neutral and screw the cable adjuster "E" in or out as necessary to bring the gear shifter to the position shown at "N" in Fig. Z12. The measurement from the machined face of the cover to the end of the gear shifter outer tube will then be 3/16in. Tighten the pinch screw "D," making sure that there is a little clearance between the locking arm and the gear shifter. Lack of clearance may result in the clutch being held partly out of engagement, so causing clutch slip when the starting lever is operated.

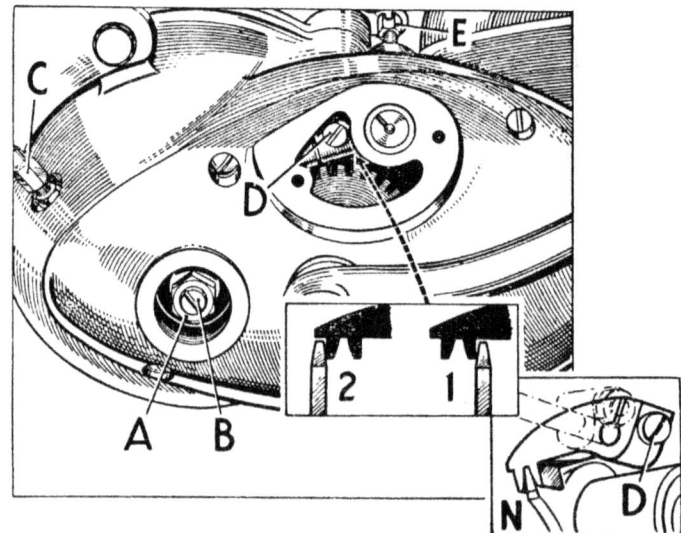

Fig. Z12. Adjusting Clutch and Pre-Selector.

Replace the rear wheel and check the engagement of both gears. It may be found necessary to alter the cable adjustment slightly either way to obtain positive selection.

Finally, refill the gearbox with ⅓ pint (190 c.c.) of the correct grade of oil (40 S.A.E.). This will bring the level up to the lower edge of the hole provided for clutch pushrod adjustment. Re-fit the starting lever and tighten the pinch bolt.

B.S.A. MOTOR CYCLES LTD.,
Service Department, Armoury Road,
Birmingham, 11.
Printed in England

BSA SERVICE SHEET No. 906

June 1957
Reprinted November 1962

Dandy 70

REMOVAL OF WHEELS, ADJUSTING, DISMANTLING, AND RE-ASSEMBLING HUBS AND BRAKES

FRONT WHEEL REMOVAL AND REPLACEMENT

Screw in the brake cable adjuster and disconnect the cable from the operating lever. Alternatively, the lever itself may be taken off by unscrewing the nut "A," Fig. Z13, from the cam spindle. If a speedometer is fitted, detach the cable by unscrewing the union nut from the drive gearbox. Do not lose the fibre washer from inside the nut.

Take off the wheel spindle nut "B" and pull out the spindle "C." Support the weight of the wheel and withdraw it from the forks, first moving it over towards the right to disengage the brake anchor pin from the suspension arm. Be careful not to damage the speedometer gearbox (if fitted). This is not fixed to the hub, and it can be lifted away as soon as the wheel is clear of the forks.

Replace the wheel by reversing the order of the above instructions. When re-fitting the speedometer gearbox, the driving arm must be located in the hole provided for it in the hub flange.

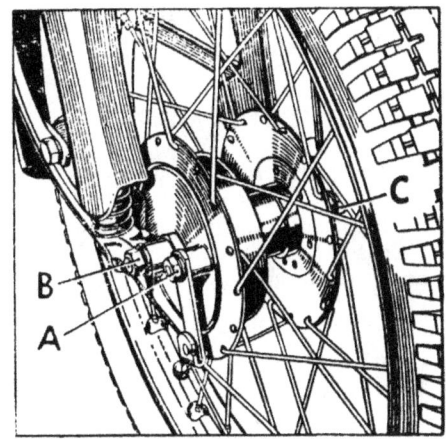

Fig. Z13. Front Wheel Removal

It is important that the brake anchor pin should be correctly engaged with the suspension arm.

REAR WHEEL REMOVAL AND REPLACEMENT

Slacken the lower bolt "A," Fig. Z14, which secures the brake anchor strap to the fork end, and disengage the strap from the peg in the brake plate. Remove the brake operating rod adjusting nut. Unscrew one of the wheel spindle nuts "B," and pull out the spindle "C." Take out the spacing collar on the right-hand side, move the wheel forward as far as possible and lift the chain off the sprocket. This can be done without disconnecting the spring link. Lean the machine to one side, or raise the rear end, and withdraw the wheel.

B.S.A. Service Sheet No. 906—*continued*

Replacement is carried out in the reverse order to that for removal. Between each wheel spindle nut "B" and the fork ends there is a large washer. These washers should be positioned behind the chain adjusting screws "E" as the wheel spindle is passed through, otherwise the chain adjusters would have to be screwed right out to clear the washers.

CHAIN ADJUSTMENT

Turn the rear wheel slowly while checking the up and down movement of the chain until the tightest point is found. The total movement at this point should be ¾in. To adjust, loosen the wheel spindle nuts slightly and move the wheel backwards or forwards as necessary by means of the chain adjusting screws "E." When the correct setting has been achieved tighten the wheel spindle nuts and the locknuts on the chain adjusters.

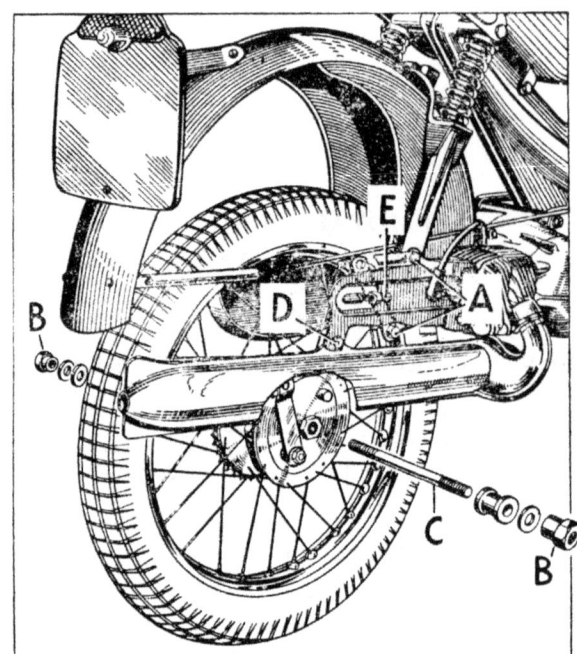

Fig. Z14. Rear Wheel Removal.

BRAKE ADJUSTMENT

The front brake is adjusted by means of the cable adjuster mounted on the right-hand suspension arm. Release the locknut "A," Fig. Z15, and turn the adjuster "B." Finally, tighten the locknut.

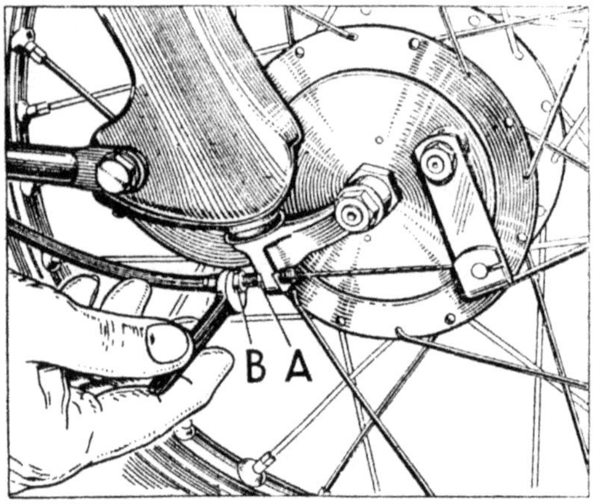

Fig. Z15. Front Brake Adjustment.

Rear brake adjustment is effected by turning the knurled nut at the end of the operating rod.

A further adjustment can be made to both brakes by moving the operating lever to a different position on the cam spindle. The spindle has a squared end, while the hole in the lever is serrated. The best position is that which results in the lever and the cable (or rod) forming a right-angle when the brake is on.

After adjusting the brakes, raise each wheel in turn clear of the ground and check that it spins freely. Binding brakes waste power and, by causing overheating, may distort the brake drums. Also, melted grease from the bearings may impregnate the brake linings.

B.S.A. Service Sheet No. 906—*continued*

WHEEL BEARING ADJUSTMENT

When the bearings are correctly adjusted, there should be about 1/64in. side play noticeable at the wheel rim. The method of adjustment is the same for both wheels.

Slacken the locknut "A", Fig. Z16, on the nearside end of the distance tube and turn the cone by means of the knurled ring "B." Fully tighten the locknut and check the side play. Too tight adjustment will cause serious damage to the bearings.

DISMANTLING THE HUBS AND BRAKES

Front and rear hubs are of similar construction; the cups, cones, ball bearings, brake shoes, springs and brake cams being identical.

Remove the locknut "A," Fig. Z16, and unscrew the adjusting cone "B." The brake assembly with the distance tube, fixed cone and locknut attached, can be withdrawn from the right-hand side of the hub. Take care not to lose the ¼in. ball bearings, of which there should be twelve in each side. The bearing cups are pressed into the hub and can be driven out with a suitable drift. When fitting new cups, ensure that they are pressed squarely into position.

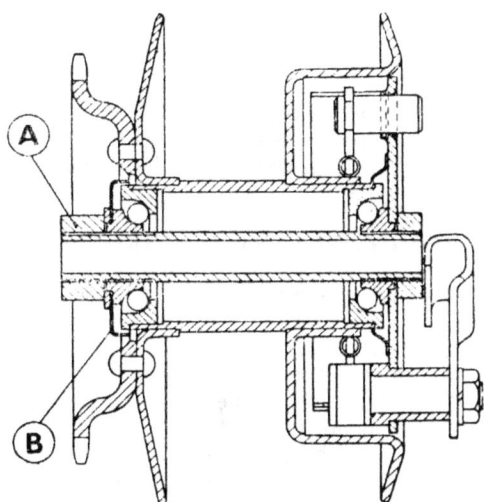

Fig. Z16. Rear Hub Arrangement.

Normal maintenance consists of cleaning out bearings and re-packing with grease at intervals of not more than 10,000 miles. If the machine is used in all weathers, or in very dusty conditions, it is wise to carry out this work more frequently.

The distance tube is detached from the brake plate by unscrewing the locknut; the fixed cone can also be unscrewed if desired. Each brake shoe is retained by a split pin and washer. When these have been removed, the shoes can be prised away from the plate until the spring tension is relieved and the ends of the shoes disengaged from the cam and fulcrum pin.

RE-ASSEMBLING

Replace the shoes in the same manner, hooking on the springs, place the ends of the shoes in position and press outwards and downwards on to the plate. Refit the retaining washers with new split pins. Brake linings should be renewed before the rivets begin to touch the drums. If the rivets are allowed to score the drums, the efficiency of the brakes can only be restored by fitting new hub shells or by having the surfaces skimmed in a lathe.

Re-assemble the bearings, using the recommended type of grease.

B.S.A. MOTOR CYCLES LTD.,
Service Department, Armoury Road,
Birmingham, 11.
Printed in England.

BSA SERVICE SHEET No. 907

Dandy 70

FRAME AND FORKS

The front forks are of the leading link type and require no adjustment. The only maintenance necessary is lubrication of the suspension arm bushes every 1,000 miles by applying a grease gun to the nipples provided, as shown in Fig. Z17.

DISMANTLING THE FORKS

Remove the front wheel as described in Service Sheet No. 906. Detach the brake cable from the right-hand suspension arm by unscrewing the adjuster. Take out the two pivot bolts, which also secure the mudguard stay. Unscrew the two bolts holding the upper ends of the fork springs. These will be found inside the legs of the forks. The arms with springs attached can then be taken away. If it is desired to change the springs, they can simply be unscrewed from the scrolls formed on the arms. The top scrolls are screwed out in a similar manner.

The pivot bearings in the arms are composed of a bush and distance tube, with a dust cap at each end of the bush.

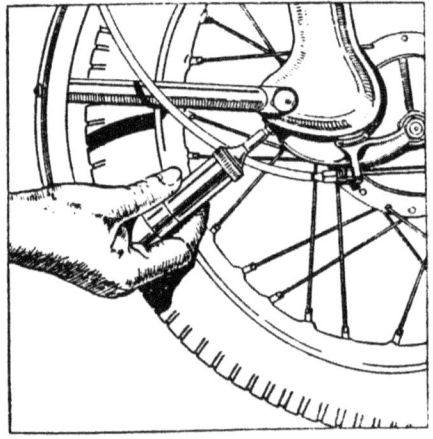

Fig. Z17. Greasing Front Forks.

RE-ASSEMBLING THE FORKS

Screw the springs firmly on to the top and bottom scrolls. Pass each spring up inside the fork legs and replace the top bolt. Assemble the pivot bearings in the arms and guide them into position, using a suitable piece of rod for lining up with the bolt holes.

STEERING HEAD ADJUSTMENT

With the front wheel clear of the ground, test for play by grasping the handlebars as shown in Fig. Z18 and attempting to rock the steering head up and down. If any play is present, the bearings require adjustment.

Slacken the locknut "B," Fig. Z19, and turn the adjusting nut "C" until the play has been taken up. Do not over-tighten or the steering will be stiff, and the ball races may be damaged. Tighten the locknut firmly.

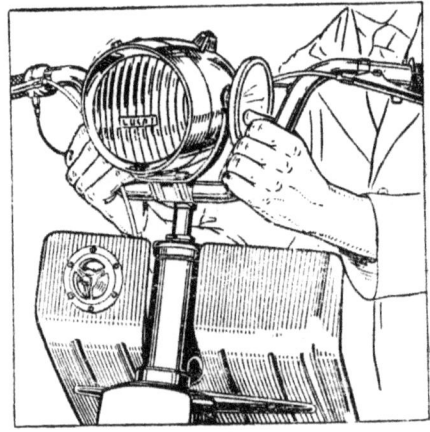

Fig. Z18. Checking Steering Head.

B.S.A. Service Sheet No. 907—*continued*

DISMANTLING THE STEERING HEAD

Remove the front wheel, as described in Service Sheet No. 906. Unscrew the bolt "A," Fig. Z19, a few turns and tap it down to release the handlebar stem expander cone. Pull the handlebars up out of the steering head. Take off the two nuts "B" and "C" while supporting the weight of the forks. Then, lower the forks until the steering column is clear of the frame. Take care not to lose any of the ball bearings; there should be twenty-four 3/16in. balls in the upper cup, and twenty ¼in. balls in the lower cup.

These bearings require cleaning out and re-packing with grease at intervals of approximately 10,000 miles.

RE-ASSEMBLING THE STEERING HEAD

Re-assemble the bearings, using fresh grease, and adjust as described above. Replace the front wheel and handlebars. Line up the latter squarely with the wheel and tighten the bolt "A" securely.

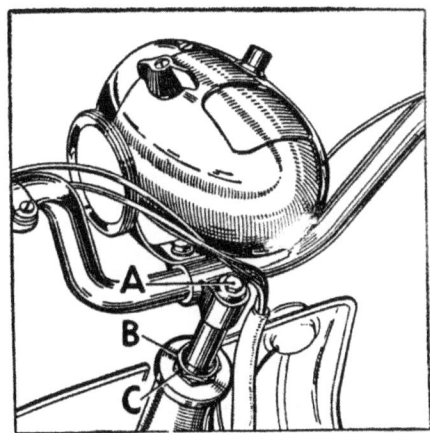

Fig. Z19.
Steering Head Adjustment.

THE REAR FORKS

The lower extremities of the rear forks are held by two bolts on each side to the chain case and swinging arm plate. The two suspension springs are mounted on top of the forks by means of special fixing plates and nuts and bolts. No lubrication or adjustment is necessary.

The bushes on which the engine and rear forks pivot are of the rubber silentbloc type. These require no attention and have an extremely long life.

WHEEL ALIGNMENT

At intervals, and particularly after the rear wheel has been moved, the alignment of the wheels should be checked. Set the front wheel straight ahead and place a long straight edge alongside the two wheels. It should touch the tyres in two places on each wheel simultaneously.

An even more accurate method is to measure the distances between the straight edge and the rims at the front and rear of each wheel, since the sides of the tyres may not always be perfectly true. These measurements should all equal.

If the wheels prove to be out of line, it may be that one of the chain adjusters has been screwed in or out more than the other. If this point is in order, then the result must lie in the frame or forks and they should be returned to a B.S.A. Dealer for checking over.

B.S.A. MOTOR CYCLES LTD.,
Service Department, Armoury Road,
Birmingham. 11,
Printed in England

BSA SERVICE SHEET No. 908

August 1958.

Dandy 70

TECHNICAL DATA

Petrol tank capacity	6 pints
Bore	45 mm.
Stroke	44 mm.
Capacity	69.9 c.c.
Compression ratio	7.25—1
Piston ring gap	min. .009″ max. .013″
Piston clearance (base of skirt)	min. .003″ max. .0048″
Contact breaker gap	Lucas .015″ Wico Pacy .018″
Ignition timing (piston before T.D.C. points just opening)	5/32″
Spark plug	Champion L7
Plug points gap	min. .018″ max. .020″
Gear ratios	Top 9.7 First 21.2
Wheel rims	G.5–J
Tyres size	20″ × 2½″
*Tyre pressures	Front 18 lbs. p.s.i. Rear 24 lbs. p.s.i.
Chain size	½″ × 3/16″ × 60 pitches
Teeth on rear chainwheel	27
Gearbox sprocket	13
Total front wheel movement	2½″
Total rear wheel movement	2½″
Brake dimensions	4″ dia. × 7/8″ wide
Carburetter bore	1/2″
Main jet	35 c.c.
Throttle valve	3
Needle position	3
Needle Jet	.0745″
Air cleaner	Amal

*Based on rider's weight of 140 lbs., for heavier load add 2 lbs. per 14 lb. increase for front and 4 lbs. per 14 lbs. increase for rear.

B.S.A. MOTOR CYCLES LTD.,
Service Dept., Birmingham, 11.
Printed in England.

WIRING WIPAC DIAGRAM

B.S.A. DANDY SEVENTY LIGHT SCOOTER
MODELS PRODUCED FROM OCTOBER 1956 TO APRIL 1957

WIPAC GROUP · BUCKINGHAM · BUCKS

EQUIPMENT	Original Equipment	Replacement Spares
Ignition Generator	I.G.1493	I.G.1596
*Headlamp (less harness)	S0342	S0938
Harness (Main)	S0344	S0344
Horn and Dip Switch Harness	S0345	SEE NOTE
Horn and Dip Switch	06205	S1356
Stop and Rear Lamp (quote Bulbs required)	S0213	S0213
Leads Set (Stop and Rear Lamp)		S0822

*Speedometer not supplied by Wipac
NOTE: Now part of Main Harness S0344

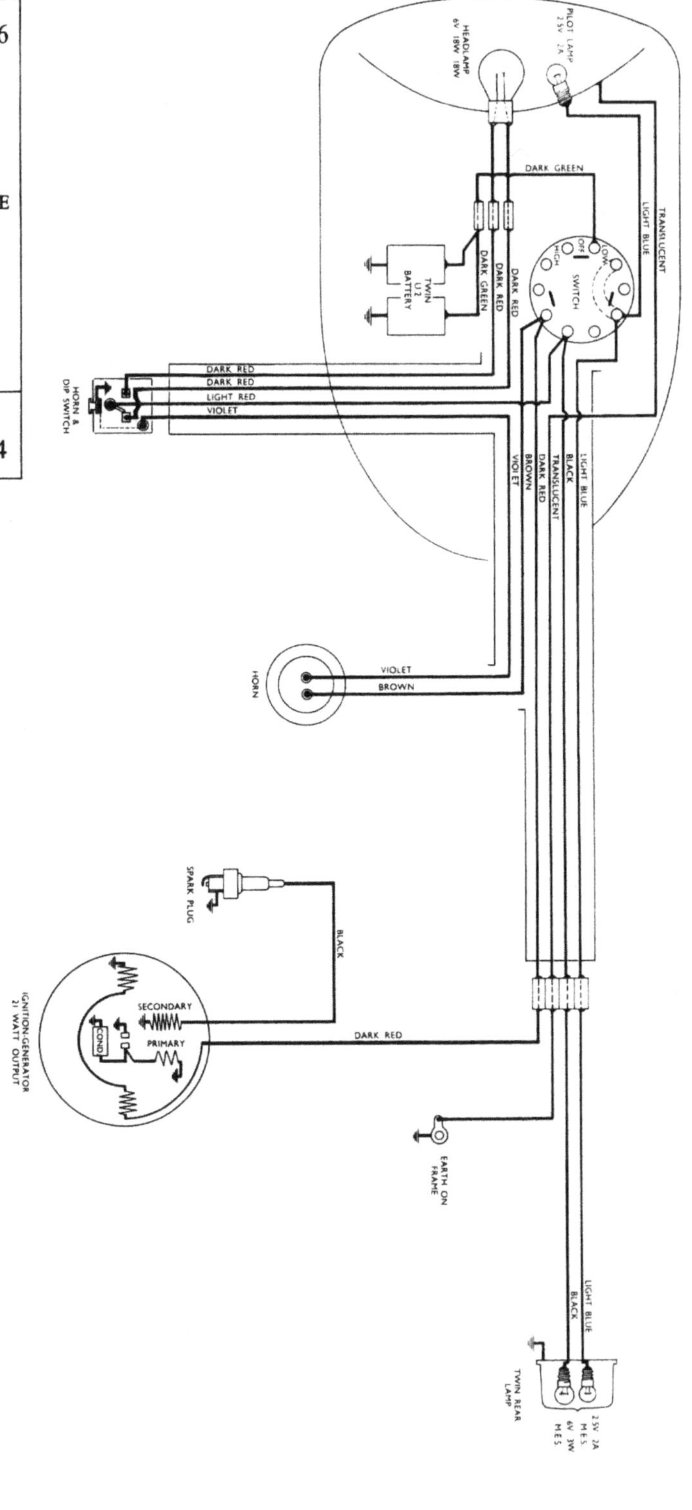

REF. WD/13/673/2

WIRING WIPAC DIAGRAM

B.S.A. DANDY SEVENTY LIGHT SCOOTER
MODELS PRODUCED FROM MAY 1957 TO JANUARY 1960

WIPAC GROUP · BUCKINGHAM · BUCKS

EQUIPMENT	Original Equipment	Replacement Spares
Ignition Generator	I.G.1501	I.G.1596
*Headlamp (less harness)	S0342	S0938
Harness (Main)	S0344	S0344
Horn and Dip Switch	06205	S1356
Stop and Rear Lamp (quote Bulbs required)	S0213	S0213
Leads Set (Stop and Rear Lamp)		S0822

*Speedometer not supplied by Wipac

REF. WD/15/708/1

WIRING WIPAC DIAGRAM

B.S.A. DANDY SEVENTY LIGHT SCOOTER
MODELS PRODUCED FROM FEB. 1960

THE WIPAC GROUP · BUCKINGHAM · BUCKS

Ref. WD/65/673

EQUIPMENT	PART No.
Ignition Generator	I.G.1596
*Headlamp (less harness)	S0938
Harness (Main)	S0344
Horn and Dip Switch	S0613
Stop and Rear Lamp (quote Bulbs required)	S0213
Leads Set (Stop and Rear Lamp)	S0822

*Speedometer not supplied by Wipac

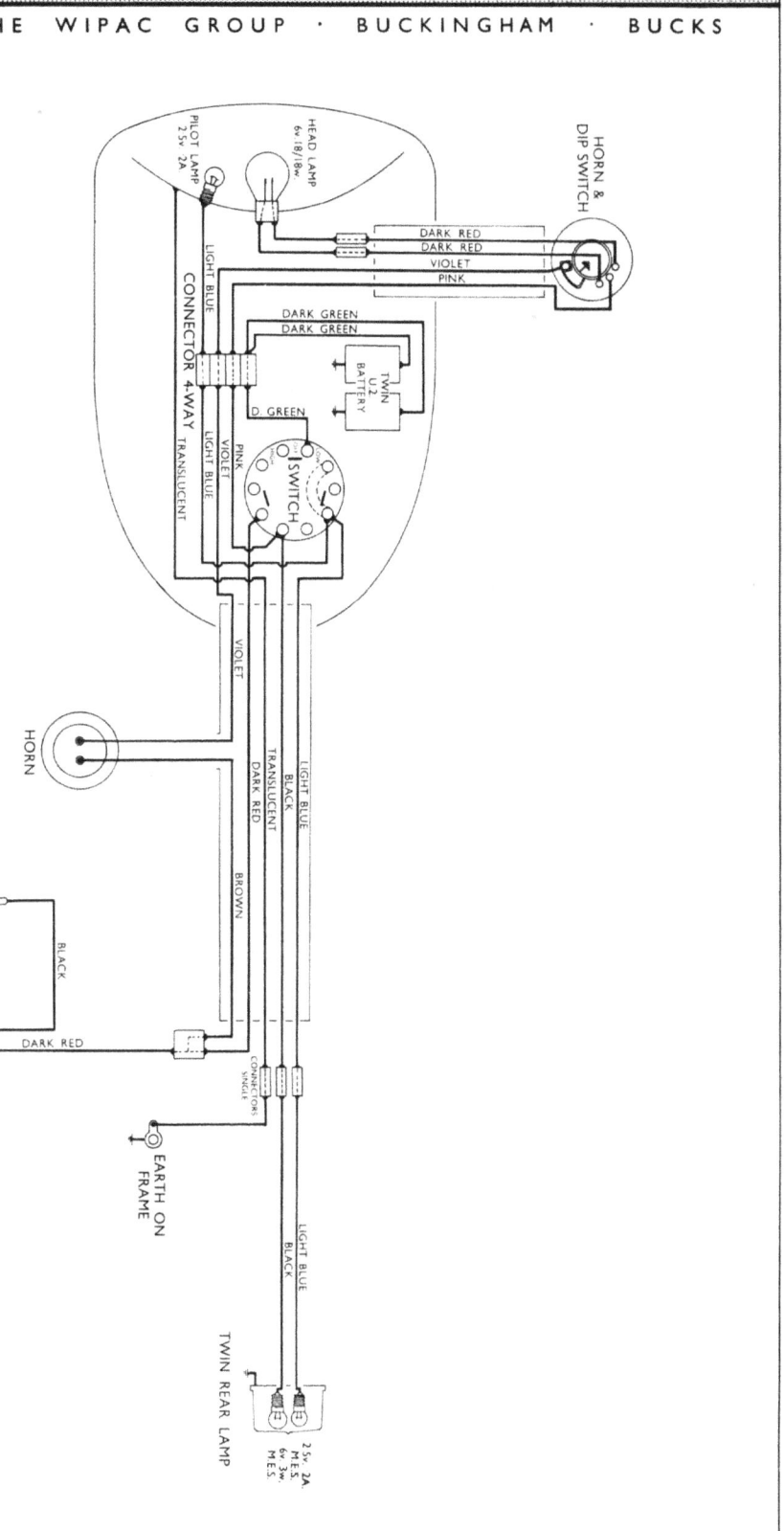

NOTES

How to ride the BSA Dandy 70

NOTES

Part One

THE CONTROLS

RIDING INSTRUCTIONS

ROUTINE MAINTENANCE

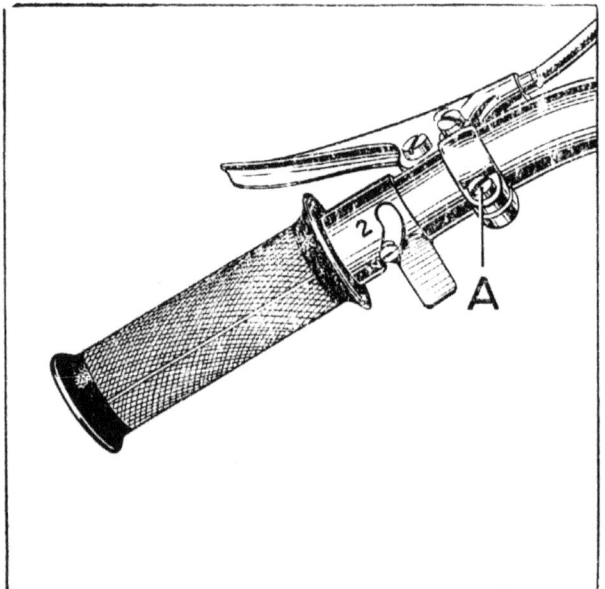

Fig. 1.

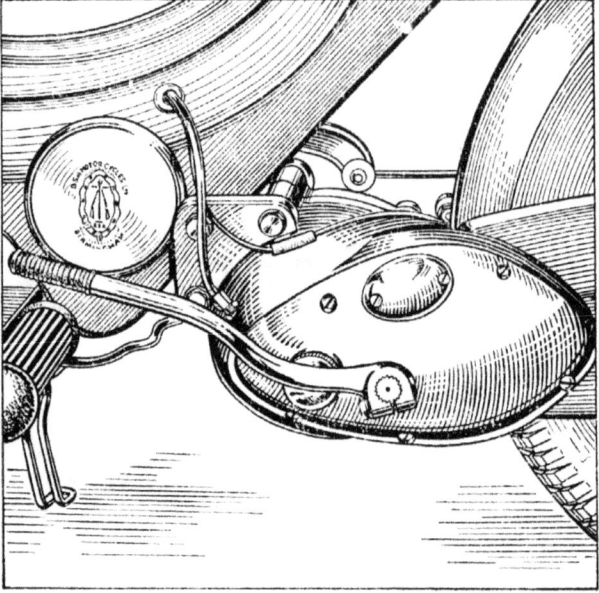

Fig. 2.

ADJUSTING THE CONTROLS

Before attempting to ride the machine set the handlebar controls to your liking. These are adjustable, being clipped to the bar as shown, and can be moved to the position most suited to your requirements by slackening off the screw A, and re-tightening afterwards.

Badly placed levers mean poor control of the machine, and can bring discomfort on long journeys.

CONTROLS ON THE LEFT SIDE OF THE MACHINE

The only control on the left hand side of the machine is the long hand lever for starting the engine.

This is operated by grasping with the left hand and pulling smartly upwards.

CONTROLS ON THE LEFT HANDLEBAR

The twist grip A operates the gear selection. It has three positions which are seen clearly in the illustration.

    1.   For LOW gear
    N.   For NEUTRAL
    2.   For HIGH gear.

Moving the twist grip to one of these positions pre-selects the gear indicated, but it is not actually engaged until the clutch is operated.

The lever B in front of the twist grip is for operating the clutch. When it is squeezed towards the bar the clutch is disengaged and the drive to the rear wheel disconnected. The clutch is re-engaged when the lever is released. This lever also automatically operates the gear change. (See Driving, page 7.)

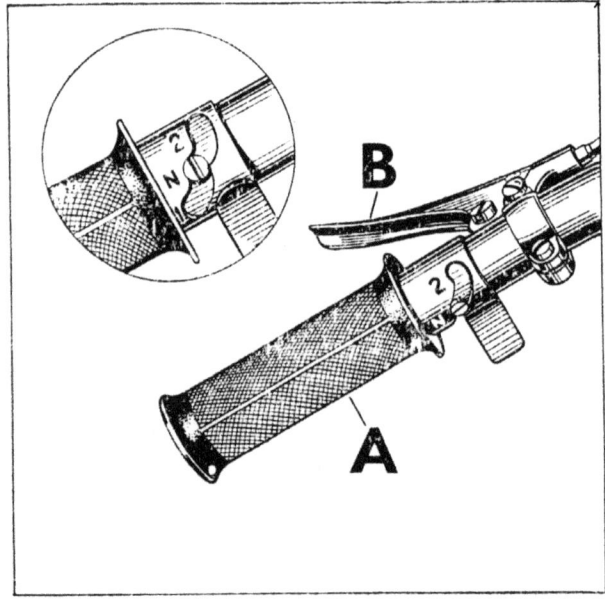

Fig. 3.

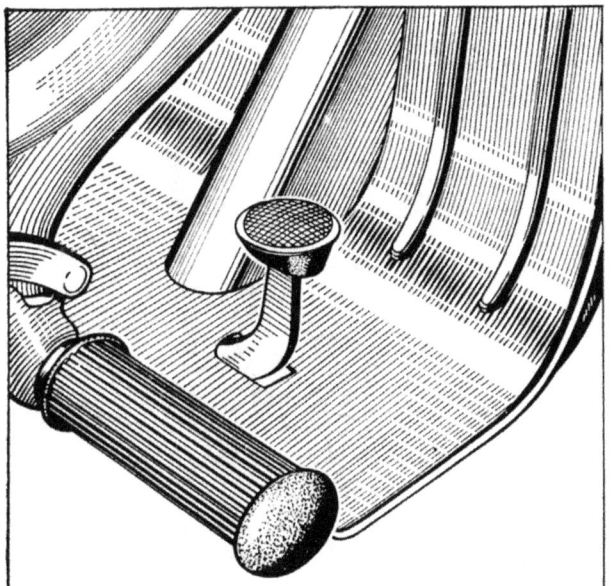

Fig. 4.

CONTROLS ON THE RIGHT SIDE OF THE MACHINE

The only control on the right hand side of the machine is the rear brake pedal, which is toe operated. Note that this does not apply both brakes — only the rear.

CONTROLS ON THE RIGHT HANDLEBAR

The twist grip A operates the carburetter throttle. To open, (i.e. to increase the engine speed), turn the grip in the direction shown by the arrow. To close, turn in the opposite direction. The total movement from throttle closed to throttle fully open is a quarter of a turn.

The hand lever B mounted in front of the twist grip is for the front brake. To operate squeeze the lever towards the bar. This lever is adjustable for position.

Also mounted on right of handlebar is the horn button C.

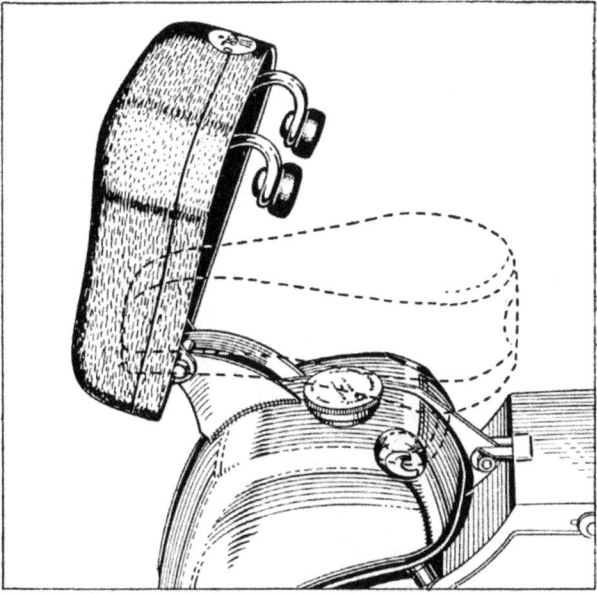

Fig. 5.

FUEL SUPPLY

The fuel tank (fill with petroil as described on page 14), is mounted at the rear of the frame under the saddle and the filler cap has a quick release bayonet fastening. To fill the tank hinge the saddle forward as shown.

The tap under the tank is opened when the knob is pulled out and turned in a clockwise direction to lock it into position. To shut off the petroil turn the knob anti-clockwise to unlock it and then push in.

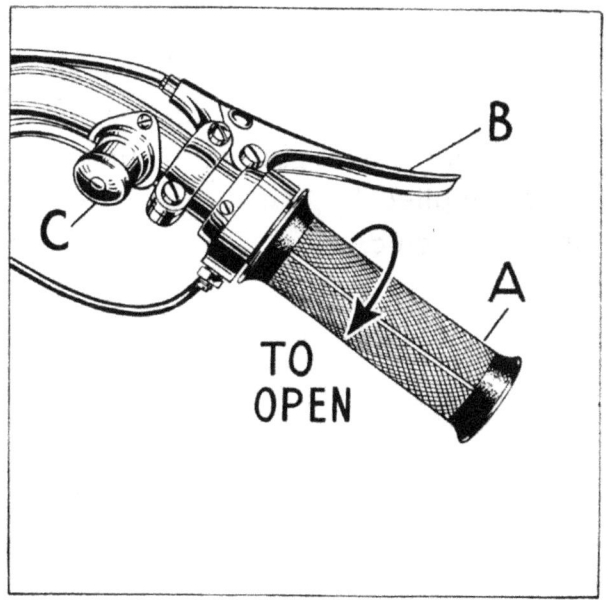

Fig. 6.

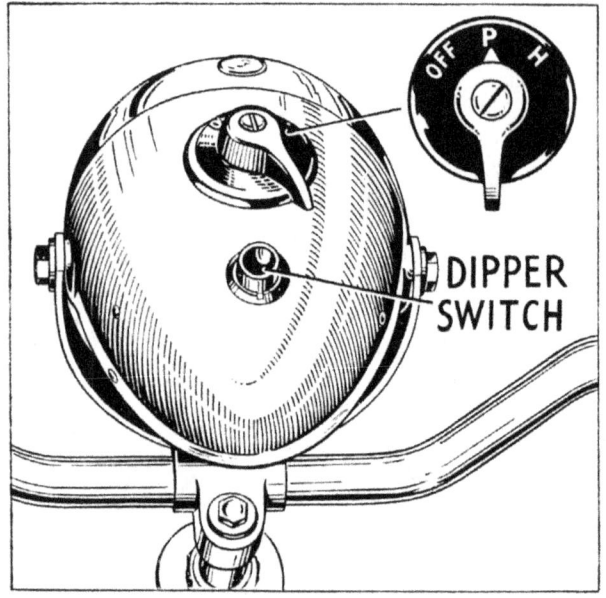

Fig. 7.

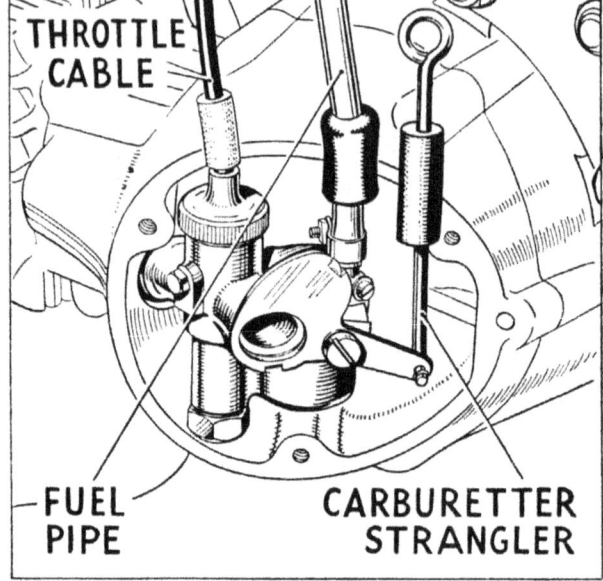

Fig. 8.

HEADLAMP SWITCH

This is built into the top of the headlamp. It has three positions.

OFF — all lights switched off.

P — this switches on the parking lights, the current being supplied by a dry battery located inside the headlamp body behind the reflector.

H — this switches on the main headlamp and the tail lamp, for use when riding at night, the current being supplied by the dynamo built into the engine.

THE CARBURETTER

The carburetter is accommodated in a special compartment built into the crankcase and it is protected by a detachable cover which incorporates a gauze air filter. Projecting from the carburetter compartment are the following items.

1. The fuel pipe from the tank under the saddle.

2. The throttle control cable which is operated by the twist grip on the right handlebar.

3. The strangler control. This is a metal eyelet which when pulled up closes the strangler, and is only used for starting *when the engine is cold*. As soon as the engine starts the strangler must be opened again by pushing the strangler control downwards to its normal position.

TO START THE ENGINE.

Set the gear in neutral by placing the gear selector twist grip in the position marked "N" and operating the clutch lever once. If cold, close the strangler. Open the twist grip control a small amount and give the handstart lever a sharp pull, whereupon the engine should fire at once. During normal running the strangler must always be kept fully open and it should be opened immediately the engine fires, or should the weather be cold, at the earliest possible moment.

Note : While it is necessary to close the strangler when starting from cold, this may not be necessary when the engine is warm and should certainly not be so if the engine is re-started after a short wait only.

TO STOP THE ENGINE.

Close the throttle and disengage the clutch. If the engine does not stop it indicates that the throttle is not closing properly. Always turn off the fuel, or better still, turn off a few seconds before stopping the engine.

TO OPERATE THE PRE-SELECTOR GEARS.

To Engage Low Gear. To engage low gear turn the left hand twist grip to the position marked "1" and de-clutch by squeezing the clutch lever towards the bar. This will automatically engage low gear, but the scooter will remain stationary until the clutch is released.

To Move Off. Open the throttle slightly by turning the right hand twist grip, and gently release the clutch lever. The scooter will begin to move forward and as soon as this happens open the throttle a little further to gain speed.

To Change Up. As soon as the scooter reaches a speed of about 10 m.p.h. change into high gear by moving the left hand twist grip to the position marked "2" and de-clutch. The gears will then automatically change to the high gear position and the clutch lever should then be immediately released. A quick and sweeter change will be obtained if the throttle twist grip is closed momentarily during this operation, but this is not absolutely essential.

To Change Down. Changing down to low gear becomes necessary when steep hills are encountered or when traffic conditions call for low speeds and rapid acceleration. Low gear is also required for starting from rest. To change to low gear turn the left hand twist grip to the position marked "1" and de-clutch, immediately re-engaging the clutch by releasing the lever. This will automatically engage low gear, and it should be noted that it is unnecessary in this case to close the throttle momentarily. It is in fact preferable not to alter the throttle opening until low gear is engaged. **IMPORTANT:** Do not engage low gear if the Dandy is exceeding 10 m.p.h. This is especially important if low gear is preselected and the clutch is operated in an emergency, such as avoiding a dog, etc.

To Select Neutral. Turn the left hand twist grip to the position marked "N", de-clutch and then immediately release the clutch lever. Avoid sharp acceleration and braking, particularly on wet roads. Always use both brakes together and apply them smoothly and progressively. Try to anticipate the need to change gear or brake so that your riding is not jerky or untidy. Maintain a natural riding position as this provides maximum control and prevents discomfort on long journeys.

RUNNING IN A NEW MACHINE.

The rider who has just purchased a new machine for the first time will do well to remember that all the hidden working parts are just as new as the enamel and plating which he can see, and that they must not be overloaded until they are well run-in.

This running-in is really the most important period in the life of the engine, and the handling you give it during the first 1,000 to 1,500 miles will determine what sort of service it is going to give you later.

It is advisable not to exceed half throttle in any gear during the first 500 miles. The Dandy's best performance will then not disappoint you. If you try to put it through its paces too soon you will run the risk of seizure and other trouble which may have a lasting effect on the engine and, in any case, until it is really run-in it will not be at its best.

Avoid sudden and sharp acceleration, especially when the engine is not pulling under load.

Do not force it up hills in top gear, when a change down would ease the load.

CLEANING THE DANDY.

Regular and thorough cleaning will obviously keep your scooter looking smart and will help to retain both its new appearance and its value. It also helps to lengthen its life and maintain efficiency if the cleaning process is carried out correctly.

Take special care to prevent dust and grit from working into such parts as hubs, carburetter, brakes and gearbox.

To rub dry and caked mud from the frame or mudguards means that the enamel on these parts will be subjected to an abrasive action which will quickly destroy the polish. Soak the mud first, and then float it off with copious supplies of clean water supplied either with a hose or a sponge. If a hose is used, take care not to direct the stream of water directly on to the engine, hubs or brakes.

When all dirt is removed, dry and polish off with a clean duster.

The engine and gearbox are best cleaned with a brush and paraffin, and then dried off with a clean rag.

ROUTINE MAINTENANCE

Fig. 9.

TYRE PRESSURES

Check the tyre pressures weekly with a proper tyre gauge as shown.

The correct recommended pressures are as follows :
   Front Tyre :   18 lb. per sq. in.
   Rear Tyre :   24 lb. per sq. in.
(Note : the above pressures are for normal riders of about 10 stone (140

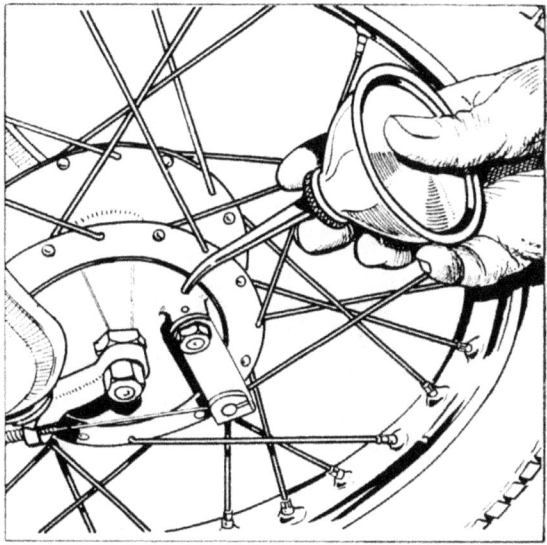

Fig. 10.

OILING THE CYCLE PARTS

Give a few drops of oil weekly to all exposed joints and cables. Use ordinary cycle oil for this purpose.

---

lb.) Heavier riders should inflate up to 4 lb. above these figures, and light riders of 7 or 8 stone can safely run with about 2 lb. less pressure).

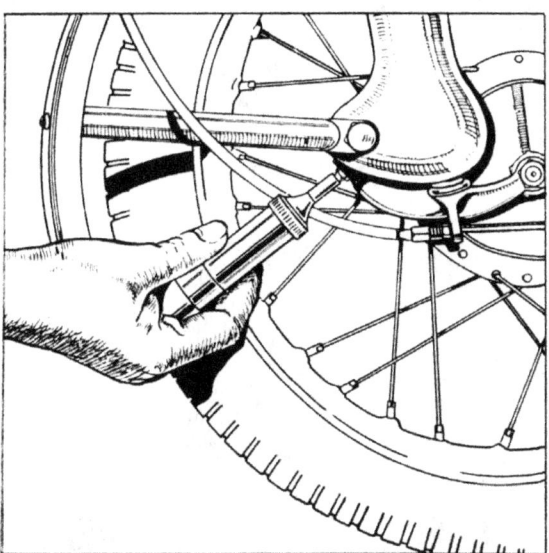

Fig. 11.

THE GREASE GUN

Give a few strokes of the grease gun every 1,000 miles to the front forks.

For the correct grades of grease, see page 11.

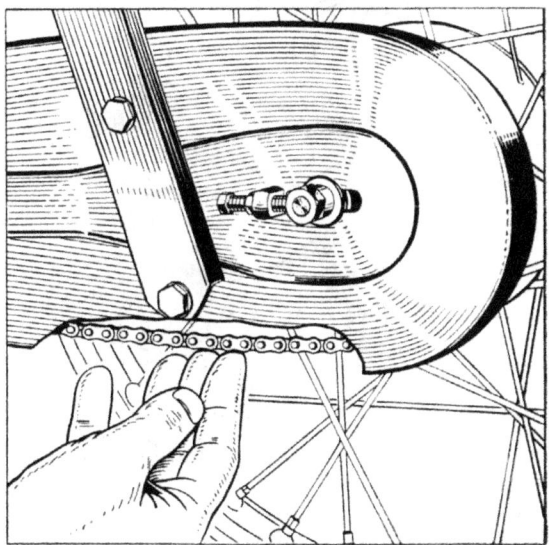

Fig. 12.

CHECKING CHAIN TENSION

Check the driving chain adjustment every 1,000 miles by feeling the free up and down movement as shown. This should amount to **not more than $\frac{3}{4}$ inch**. If incorrect, adjust as described on page 25.

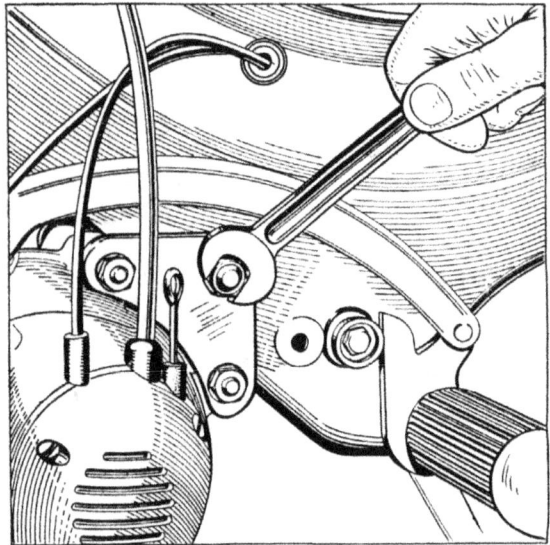

Fig. 13.

CHECKING NUTS AND BOLTS

Check that all nuts are tight every 2,000 miles. They are not likely to work loose, but this is a wise precaution and well worth the small amount of time and trouble involved.

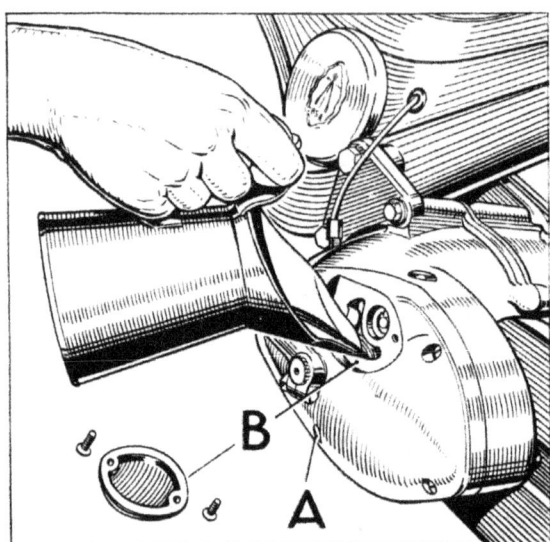

Fig. 14.

TOPPING-UP GEARBOX

Drain and refill the gearbox every 2,000 miles.

Remove the bottom screw A to drain, and replace before pouring in fresh oil through orifice B. Approximate capacity $\frac{1}{3}$ pint (190 c.c.).

For correct grades see page 11.

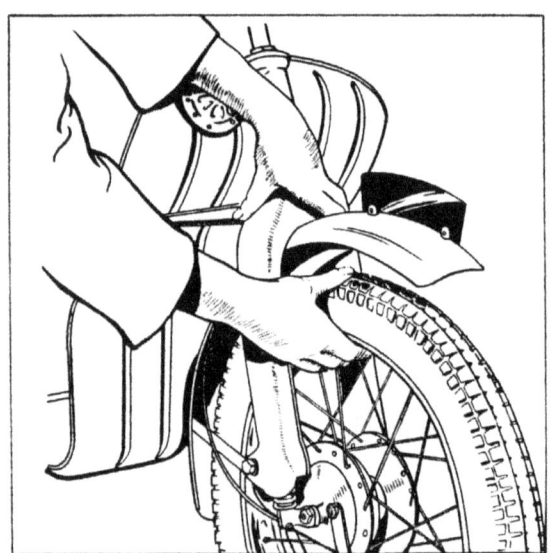

Fig. 15.

CHECKING WHEEL BEARINGS

Check hub adjustment every 2,000 miles by raising the wheel clear of the ground, and feeling the shake at the rim. If there is no shake the adjustment is set too tight, but it must not exceed about 1/64th inch, (i.e. just perceptible). If incorrect adjust as described on page 24.

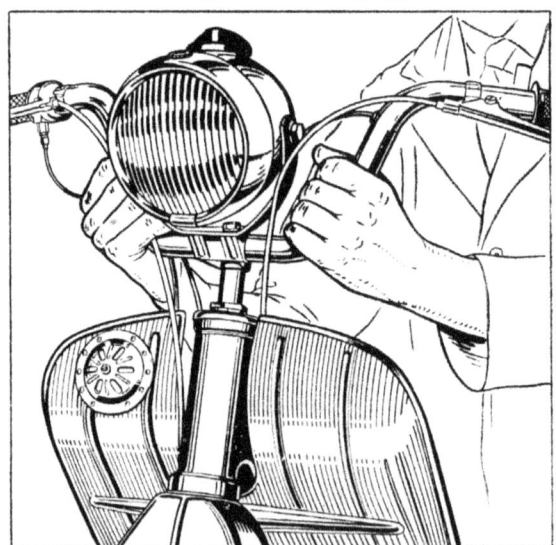

Fig. 16.

CHECKING STEERING HEAD

Test for play every 2,000 miles by feeling for shake as shown in the illustration. If there is no shake the adjustment is set too tight, but it must not exceed about 1/64th inch, (i.e. just perceptible). If incorrect adjust as described on page 27.

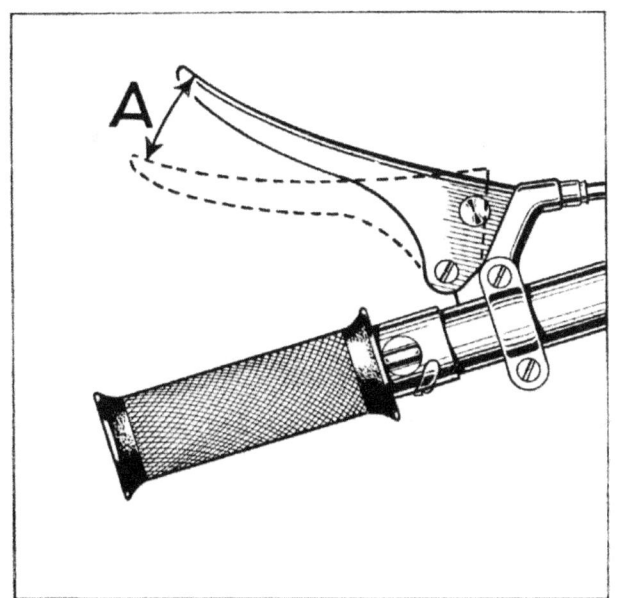

Fig. 17.

CLUTCH ADJUSTMENT (HANDLEBAR)

The clutch must be in full engagement when the lever is released, and completely free in the disengaged position. To ensure this see that there is sufficient free movement at the lever as shown in the illustration at A. This play should not be less than $\frac{1}{8}$th inch. If incorrect adjust as described on page 22.

RECOMMENDED LUBRICANTS
(Summer and Winter)

Mix one of the following Oils with petrol in the ratio of 1 : 20 unless otherwise shown.

BRAND	OIL		GREASE POINTS
	ENGINE	GEARBOX	
Wakefield	Castrol Two-Stroke Oil (1:16) or Castrol XXL	Castrol XXL	Castrolease Heavy
Shell	Shell-BP Petroiler Mix No. 1. or Shell X-100 40	Shell X-100 40	Shell Retinax A
Esso	Esso Two-Stroke Motor Oil (1:16) or Essolube 40	Esso Extra Motor Oil 40/50	Esso High Temperature Grease
Mobil	MobilMix TT (1:16) or Mobiloil BB	Mobiloil D	Mobilgrease MP
BP	Shell-BP Petroiler Mix No. 1 or Energol SAE 40	Energol SAE 40	Energrease C3

NOTES

Part Two

GENERAL INSTRUCTIONS FOR

LUBRICATION

ADJUSTMENTS

DECARBONISATION

OVERHAUL, ETC.

Lubrication. Lubrication for the engine is provided by oil dissolved in the petrol to provide a mixture commonly called "petroil". The filler cap on top of the petrol tank will be found to incorporate a tubular extension which projects into the tank. This serves as a measure for the lubricating oil and is used for preparing the correct mixture of petrol and oil required. The correct proportion of oil to petrol is given on page 11. The grades of oil recommended on page 11 should be used, as lighter grades will prove unsuitable.

For correct running of the engine and also for adequate lubrication, it is essential that the oil should be completely dissolved in the petrol, and it is, therefore, preferable to mix the two in a separate container before pouring into the tank. If this is not possible however, as for instance, when obtaining petrol from a wayside pump, the oil should be put into the petrol after filling up with the latter and the machine should be shaken thoroughly to ensure correct mixing of the two liquids. If this is not done, there is the risk of liquid oil undiluted with petrol lying at the bottom of the tank, reaching the carburetter and clogging the fuel supply system. As the only lubrication for the engine is by means of fuel drawn in through the carburetter the scooter must not be coasted downhill for long periods with the throttle shut as the engine may suffer seizure through lack of lubrication.

Ignition Timing and Contact Breaker. The ignition timing is accurately set within very close limits during assembly of the engine at the factory, and in common with other two-stroke engines it is of the fixed type without manual or automatic control.

Any variation in timing can only be secured by moving the stator housing (Fig. 18, page 15) or the rocker arm C, Fig. 18. The former can be rotated through a very small angle by releasing the two screws A, not forgetting to re-tighten them after the adjustment has been completed. This can only be accomplished when the engine is removed from the frame, (see page 17). This, however, is only intended for adjustment during original assembly and should never be touched subsequently.

The adjustment of the contact breaker points on the other hand calls for inspection at intervals, because the proper functioning of the ignition system depends upon the setting of the gap between the contact breaker points.

The contact breaker mechanism has been specially designed for long life with the result that inspection and re-adjustment of the points is not likely to become necessary at intervals of less than 5,000 miles (8,000 kilometres) as described on page 28 and this means that the operation need only be carried out at every third decarbonisation.

To adjust the Contact Breaker Points. Remove the engine from the frame as described on page 17, withdraw the flywheel, and then turn the engine shaft until the points B, Fig. 18 are fully open, and insert a feeler gauge between them. The correct gap in this position should be ·018 in. (·44 mm.) and if this is found to be wrong, release the screw D about one turn with a screwdriver and move the adjusting plate until the correct gap of ·018 in. has been restored, finally re-tightening the screw.

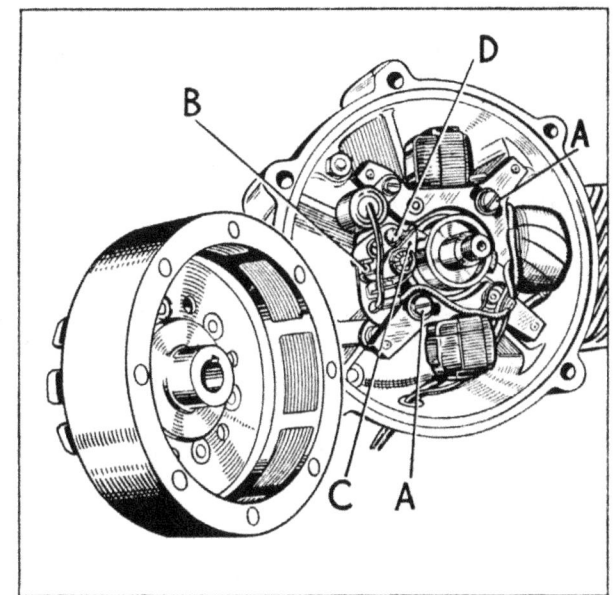

Fig. 18.   Contact Breaker Assembly.

To Check the Ignition Timing. Remove the sparking plug and turn the engine until the piston is felt to be at top dead centre, by means of a suitable rod inserted through the sparking plug hole, and then turn the engine back until the piston has descended $\frac{5}{32}$ in. (4 mm.). With the piston in this position, the contact breaker rocker arm should be commencing to rise on the contact breaker cam, and the points should have opened not more than ·002 in. (·05 mm.). If they are open more than this the timing is too far advanced. If they are open less, the timing is excessively retarded, although a small variation in either direction is not detrimental to the running of the engine.

DECARBONISATION.

Decarbonising is extremely simple and should be carried out at regular intervals of about fifteen hundred miles (2,500 kilometres) if consistent results are to be expected. The symptoms indicating an excessive deposit of carbon are undue roughness of the engine and a tendency to pink under load, erratic running with excessive four and eight stroking, and an appreciable falling off in power. This latter item is particularly noticeable when the exhaust port becomes fouled with carbon as it causes an obstruction to the free escape of the exhaust gas, and interferes with the correct scavenging of the cylinder which is so necessary for the efficient transfer of combustible mixture from the crankcase. Removal of this deposit alone may often suffice to restore the engine performance.

During the complete operation the rear end of the machine may be raised if desired. Place a length of rope under the petrol tank, and tie the ends to the shed or garage door, so lifting the rear wheel clear of the ground. Alternatively, place a box or chair on either side of the machine. Lift the machine up by inserting a length of wood or metal under the petrol tank with the ends resting on the boxes or chairs.

Silencer. It is customary to clean the baffle unit of the silencer during decarbonisation. Unscrew the union nut on the side of the cylinder barrel by means of the special " C " spanner included in the tool kit. If this nut should prove unduly obstinate, a few drops of penetrating oil should be applied to the threaded portion immediately above the nut and a little time should be allowed for this to act before attempting to unscrew the nut. Care must be taken not to lose the copper washer. This washer is important and if damaged it must be replaced with a new one. After removing the remaining bolt D, Fig. 19, the silencer can be removed.

It should then be soaked in a strong caustic solution, preferably overnight. One of the proprietary brands of cleaner recommended for gas ovens and the like may be used for this purpose. The carbon will then be freed and can be washed out with running water. (These solutions will not harm the finish of the silencer.

Removal of the Cylinder Head. The exhaust pipe must be disconnected by releasing the union nut on the side of the cylinder barrel as explained under the previous heading. Disconnect the high tension lead from the sparking plug and unscrew the latter. Remove the two bolts A, Fig. 19, on the rear fork. Take off the nuts B and withdraw the wheel spindle C a small amount.

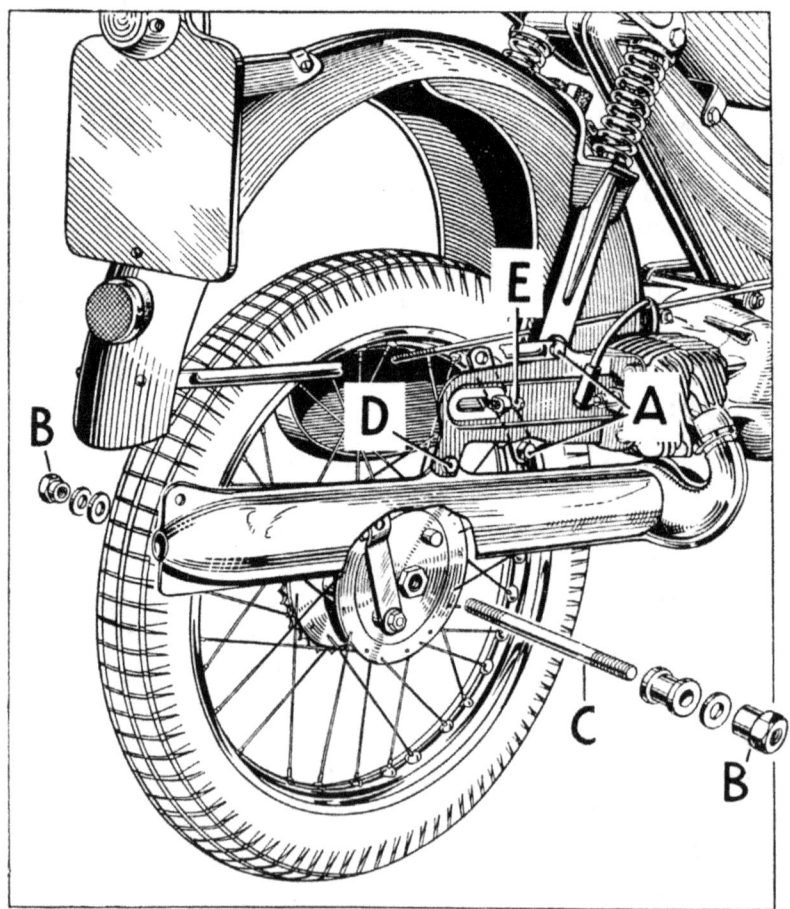

Fig. 19.   Rear Wheel Removal.

The swinging arm, cylinder head and barrel are attached to the crankcase by means of four long studs, and when the four nuts on top of the cylinder head are removed, pull the swinging arm clear so as to enable the cylinder head to be removed, being careful not to lose the four distance pieces.

The Cylinder Head, Ports and Piston. Remove all carbon deposit from the cylinder head, bearing in mind that the aluminium is soft and easily damaged if the decarbonising tool is carelessly applied, and carefully wipe clean to ensure removal of all loose particles.

Scrape off any carbon which has accumulated on the crown of the piston, taking care again not to damage the relatively soft surface of the metal itself, and after removing all the carbon, polish lightly with fine emery cloth if desired and finally wipe clean with an oily rag.

Most of the carbon deposit is likely to have accumulated in the exhaust port. Scrape this out carefully, taking care not to let the tool slip into the bore and damage the surface of the latter. Finally, wipe the exhaust port and cylinder bore absolutely clean.

Before re-assembling, smear the cylinder bore liberally with clean engine oil. (For further dismantling see below).

Removing the Engine from the Frame. Every 5,000 miles (8,000 kilometres) or third decarbonisation, it is a good idea to examine the piston and rings and the big end for wear. This is best accomplished by removing the engine from the frame. Take off the five nuts A, Fig. 20. The complete engine can then be removed and placed on a bench.

Take care when removing the barrel to support the piston as it emerges from the end of the bore in order that it may not be damaged as it falls clear.

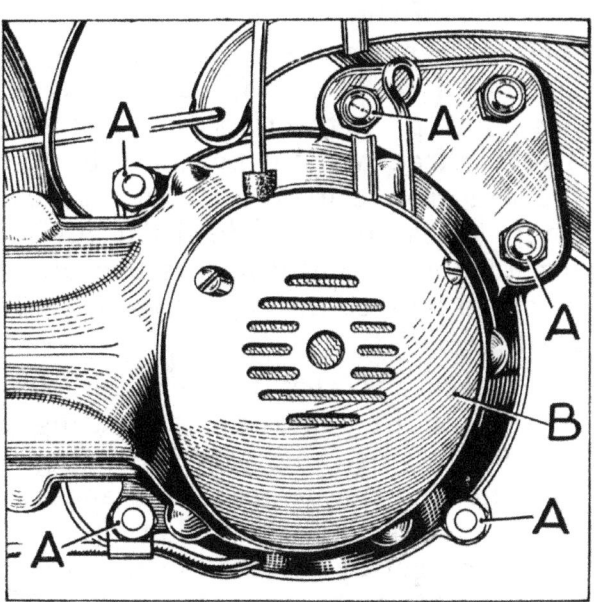

Fig. 20.   Removing Engine from Frame.

Piston. It should not be necessary to remove this from the connecting rod, but if it should be desired to do this for any reason, first remove the circlip from one end of the gudgeon pin using a pair of pointed nose pliers or some suitable instrument to lever the circlip out. Then holding the piston firmly in the hand, tap the gudgeon pin out from the other end. If it is too tight to move, it can be released by warming the piston by means of a rag soaked in hot water and wrung out. Application of this rag will cause the aluminium alloy of the piston to expand more than the steel gudgeon pin, thus releasing the latter which can then be freely pushed or tapped out.

Piston Rings. Now examine the piston rings noting that these are located in their grooves by means of pegs which engage in the piston ring gaps. If in good condition, the rings will be found to present a uniformly smooth metallic surface over their entire peripheries, and if they are in this condition and obviously have a certain amount of " springiness " as evidenced by the fact that their free gap is considerably greater than the closed gap when in the bore they should not be disturbed. If, on the other hand, the rings show signs of heat as evidenced by brown or more highly discoloured patches, they should be replaced by new rings, and in this case particular attention should be paid to the fit of the ends of the rings on their locating pegs in the piston ring grooves, and they should also be checked in the bore to ensure that they have an adequate gap. These points will not arise if genuine B.S.A. spares are fitted as the gaps on these are already correct when the rings are sent out, but if for any reason genuine B.S.A. spares are not obtainable, these points must receive careful attention. First place the ring in the cylinder bore in a position where it is clear of the ports and, making certain that it is square by pressing the skirt of the piston against it or a suitable bar of material of the correct diameter, examine the gap which should be not less than specified (see Technical Data, page 31). Having satisfied yourself on this point, place the ring in its groove on the piston and make certain that it is free without perceptible up and down play. If it is not free and the groove itself is clean, rub the ring down on a piece of fine emery cloth laid on a dead flat surface, using a rotary motion of the arm to ensure uniform pressure on the ring. As soon as the ring is found to be free in its groove, wipe it absolutely clean and fit it into position.

Check also that there is sufficient clearance between the inner portion of the gap and the locating peg in the groove. Do this by closing the ring in its groove by finger pressure until there is no gap, thus shewing that there is clearance at the peg underneath. If the gap will not close, indicating that the steps are binding on the peg, ease the steps gently with a dead smooth file. If the piston has been removed from the connecting rod refit it, first putting a smear of oil on the gudgeon pin, not forgetting a new circlip to replace the one which was removed.

The piston must be replaced in its original position — i.e., with piston ring gaps opposite the exhaust port.

Big-end Bearing. While the cylinder is off it is as well to test the big-end bearing for wear. This is done by taking hold of the connecting rod stem and pulling it upwards until the crank is at top dead centre. Then holding it in this position try gently but firmly to pull and push the connecting rod in the direction of its travel in order to feel whether there is any play. If the big-end is in a sound condition there should be no play in this direction, although it may be possible to rock the rod sideways. If vertical play is perceptible in the big-end and you do not feel qualified to decide whether the amount in evidence is permissible or not, you should seek expert advice. This point is not likely to give trouble, however, provided that the machine has been carefully used and adequately lubricated, for the big-end bearing is of ample dimensions for the work it has to do. But if for any reason the big-end bearing has deteriorated as the result of neglect or abuse, it should be replaced and unless you have the necessary experience and facilities for this class of work it is preferable to have it done by an expert repairer.

Re-assembly. Rebuild the complete engine assembly before attempting to put the unit back into the frame as follows:

Before attempting to replace the cylinder barrel over the piston smear the latter with new engine oil. Place the barrel over the piston, carefully manipulating the rings into the end of the bore, seeing that they enter freely without the application of force. As soon as the cylinder barrel is home replace the cylinder head, and the distance pieces. Refit the swinging arm and tighten down the cylinder holding nuts, doing this in diagonal order so as to avoid distortion. Examine the sparking plug and replace if sound. Re-assembly into the frame is carried out in the reverse order to dismantling. Clean the crankcase and gearcase faces carefully to remove all traces of jointing compound. Take care not to damage the soft aluminium surface. The mating surfaces should be lightly coated with jointing compound before bolting the two halves together.

Re-assembly from this point is as described under decarbonising.

Sparking Plug. The sparking plug is of great importance in satisfactory engine performance, and every care should be taken to fit the correct type when replacements are necessary. There is little to be gained by experimenting with different plugs as the make and type fitted by us as official factory equipment is best suited to the requirements of the motor. This is Champion type No. L10S, Fig. 21.

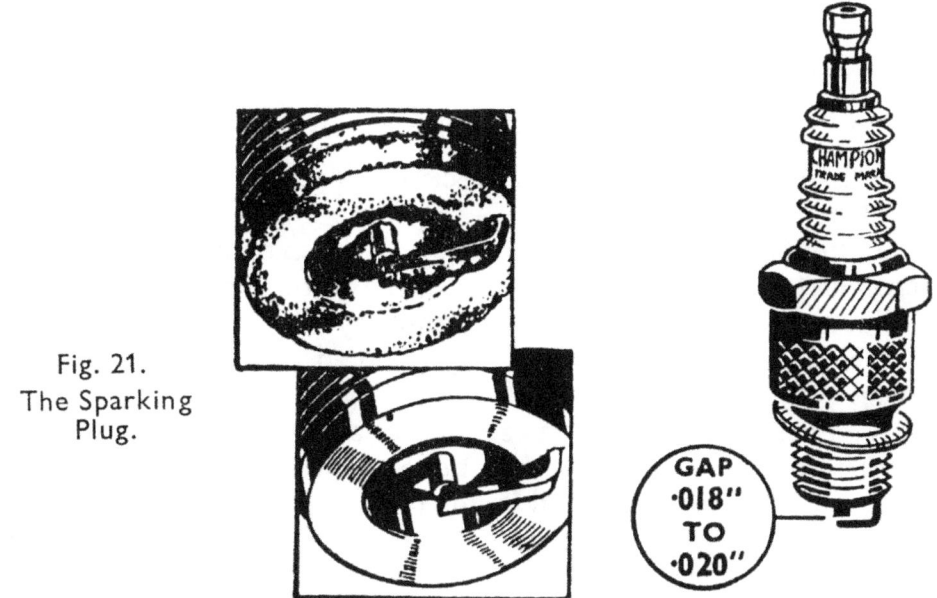

Fig. 21. The Sparking Plug.

Remove the sparking plug every 1,000 miles (1,500 kilometres) or so for inspection. If the carburation system is in correct adjustment the sparking plug points should remain clean almost indefinitely. An over-rich mixture from the carburetter will, however, cause the formation of a sooty deposit on the points and, later, on the plug end face (as upper view, Fig. 21). If therefore such a deposit is found, clean it off carefully and check your carburetter. Too high a proportion of oil in the petroil mixture will also cause plug fouling (see page 11). The continued use of leaded fuel may also eventually produce a deposit on the plug, this time of a greyish colour.

A light deposit due to any of these causes can easily be cleaned off, but if it is allowed to accumulate, particularly inside the body, the plug may spark internally with an adverse effect on engine performance if, indeed, it does not stop the engine altogether. The plug should be cleaned and tested at regular intervals, and it is suggested that this service be performed at your garage on a special " Air Blast " service unit. If eventually the cleaning process fails to restore the plug to its original condition of efficiency, it should be replaced by a new one.

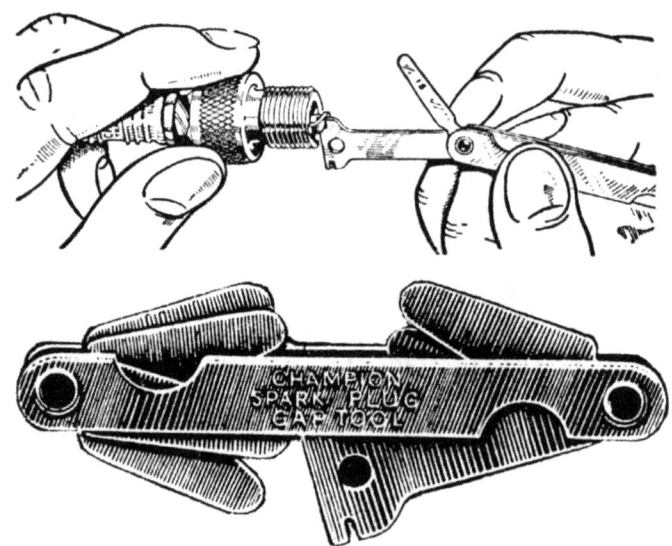

Fig. 22. Checking Plug Points.

When inspecting a plug, also check the gap between the points. This should be ·018—·020 in. (·44—·50 mm.) and adjustment should be made by bending the side wire (Fig. 22). Never attempt to move the centre electrode, and it is always advisable to use the special plug gap tool illustrated, obtainable at 2/- from any Champion Plug stockist or from the Champion Sparking Plug Co. Ltd., Feltham, Middlesex. Feeler gauges are attached to verify correct gap.

When refitting a plug, make sure that the copper washer is not defective in any way. If it has become worn or flattened, fit a new one to ensure obtaining a gastight joint.

Screw the plug down by hand as far as possible, then use a spanner for tightening only. Always use a tubular box spanner to avoid possible fracture of the insulator, and do not in any circumstances use an adjustable spanner.

Paint splashes, accumulation of grime and dust, etc., on the top half of the insulator, are often responsible for poor plug performance. The plug should be wiped frequently with a clean rag.

CARBURATION.

So long as the engine continues to run satisfactorily the carburetter is best left alone, particularly by the inexperienced rider. Access to the carburetter, however, can be obtained by taking off the cover plate B, Fig. 20, which is held in position by three screws.

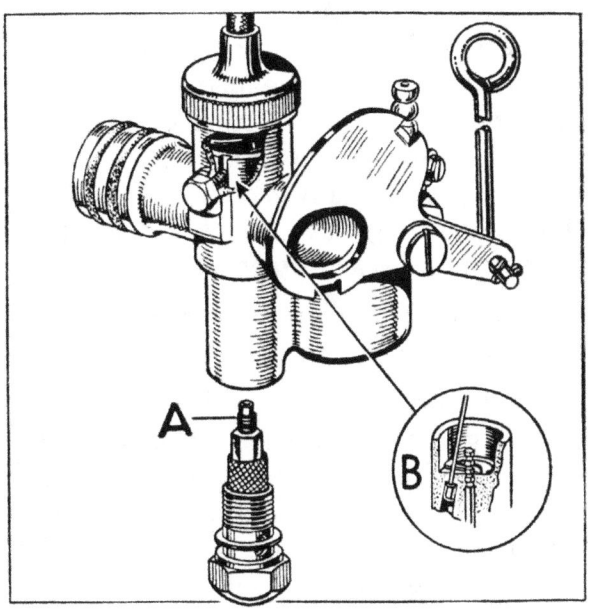

Fig. 23.   Carburetter.

The setting employed is suitable for a very wide range of climatic temperature and road conditions, and it is highly improbable that the rider will need to modify it in any way. If, however, it is felt that the conditions under which the machine is operated might permit of a slightly more economical setting this can be provided by the fitting of a smaller main jet A, Fig. 23, or by lowering the jet needle B one notch. The former alteration will supply a slightly weaker mixture throughout the entire range of throttle opening, whereas an alteration to the jet needle position has little or no effect on the full throttle setting. Conversely, the fitting of a larger main jet enriches the mixture throughout the entire range, while raising the jet needle a notch has a similar effect on intermediate throttle openings only. It is emphasised, however, that no alteration to the setting should be made except for special requirements, and only then on expert advice.

Carburetter Strangler. New riders especially are advised to study the action of the strangler and to treat this device with respect. It should only be used momentarily when starting from cold and even then only when necessary. Immediately the engine fires it should be opened.

The strangler is built into the air intake of the carburetter, and consists of a slotted plate which, when rotated, varies the amount of air admitted to the carburetter. When the strangler is closed (i.e. brought into operation by raising the wire loop seen in Fig. 8) this closes the air intake, thus reducing the air admitted to the carburetter to a minimum and providing in consequence a very rich mixture.

Air Cleaner. The gauze air cleaner built into the carburetter cover plate should be rinsed in petrol periodically, say, every time the engine is decarbonised, in order to wash away any foreign matter which has been trapped in the wire mesh, as this will upset the carburation and cause heavy petrol consumption.

TRANSMISSION.

Care of the Driving Chain. It is a good plan periodically to remove the chain, clean it thoroughly in petrol or paraffin, and then gently warm in a mixture of grease and graphite. When cool wipe off excess grease, clean sprockets and replace chain. Remember when replacing the chain which is fitted with a detachable connecting link that the spring fastener must always be put on with the closed end facing the forward direction of travel (i.e. on the top run) of the chain.

Driving Chain Adjustment. Adjustment of the chain involves moving the rear wheel and is described on page 24.

Clutch Control. The main clutch adjustment is totally enclosed in the gearbox, and is exposed when the filler plug is removed. It consists of an adjusting pin B, Fig. 24, screwed into the clutch withdrawal sleeve and a locknut A to secure it in position. This adjusting pin presses against the clutch withdrawal rod with a steel ball interposed. The withdrawal mechanism must at all times be so adjusted that there is a slight amount of play between the pin, the steel ball

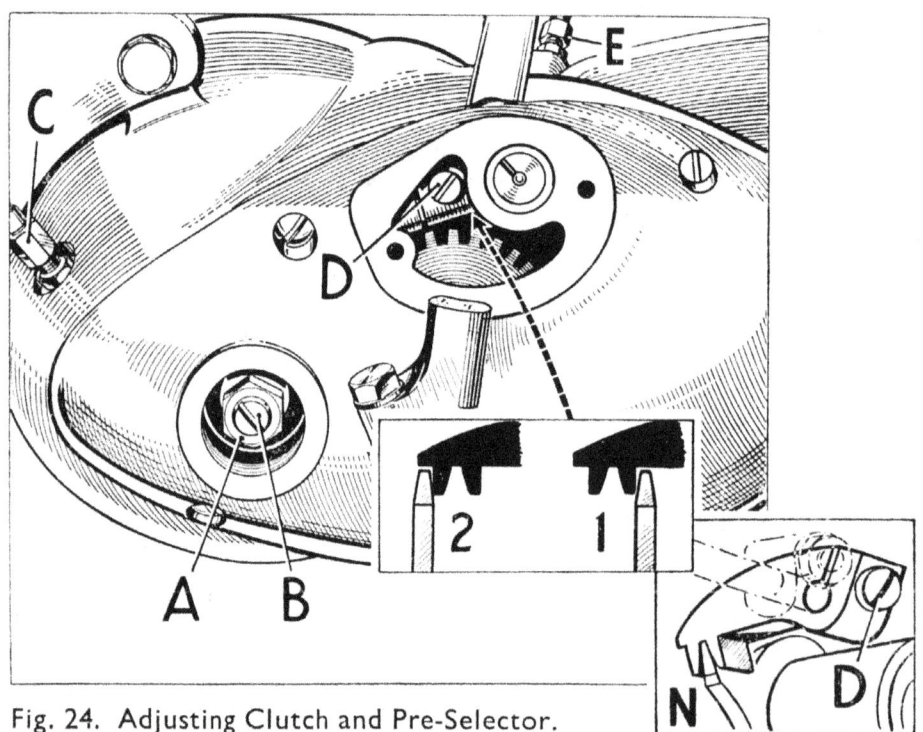

Fig. 24. Adjusting Clutch and Pre-Selector.

and the operating rod, in order that the clutch springs may exert their full pressure. If there is not sufficient play there will be a tendency for the clutch to slip continually owing to reduced spring pressure, and this in turn will cause overheating and serious damage to the clutch. If the play becomes excessive, difficulty will be experienced in changing gear, as the clutch may not fully dis-engage, in which case the control should be adjusted as explained below.

To adjust, disengage the clutch by pulling in the hand lever, and releasing the locknut A, Fig. 24. Engage the clutch and turn the adjusting pin B with a screwdriver back one or two turns. Then screw the adjusting pin in gently until it is felt to meet some resistance. Unscrew it half a turn, dis-engage the clutch and re-tighten the locknut. When this adjustment has been completed the cable should be adjusted by means of the adjuster at C until it has approximately $\frac{1}{8}$ in. free play at the handlebar end.

Clutch Dismantling. Before dismantling the clutch, the two inner crankcase and gearcase halves must be split by removing the five nuts A, Fig. 20.

Remove the spindle nuts B, Fig. 19, and the two bolts A. The complete engine unit can then be pulled away from the gearbox. With the engine removed from the frame the clutch is exposed and should be dismantled as explained below.

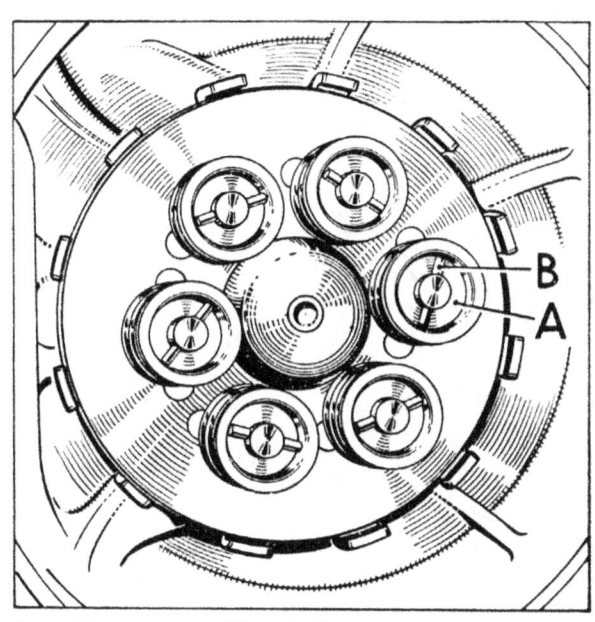
Fig. 25.   Clutch Springs.

Removal of the six cotters B, Fig. 25, after pressing down spring cups A, will enable the clutch end plate to be withdrawn. When the spring pressure plate is removed, the cork and plain clutch plates can be withdrawn. If obvious signs of glazing are present, the friction plate must be replaced. Replacement will also be necessary if the plain plates are scored. It is advisable to renew the clutch springs while the clutch is dismantled, as with continual pressure they tend to lose their springiness.

Re-assembly is carried out in the reverse order. Before joining the crankcase and gearcase together see page 19.

Gearbox. The gearbox, although built in unit construction with the engine, is self-contained as regards lubrication. Engine oil is used for lubricating the gears (see page 11). The gearbox capacity is $\frac{1}{3}$ pint (190 c.c.). When topping up the gearbox remove the filler plug (see Fig. 14), and pour engine oil in until it just reaches the level of the orifice.

To change the oil in the gearbox remove the drain screw A, Fig. 14, at the bottom of the gearbox outer cover and drain out the old oil. Wash out the gearbox with flushing oil and refill with new oil through filler hole to the correct level.

Pre-selector Gear Control. This is accurately set at the factory during assembly, and as its action is simple and straightforward it is not likely to require any attention. If for any reason such as broken or stretched Bowden control cable the mechanism requires to be re-adjusted, this should be carried out in the following manner. First slacken off pinch screw D, Fig. 24. Place the twist grip in the neutral position marked N, and disengage the clutch, whereupon the operating fork and coupling dogs should automatically move to the neutral position (see Fig. 24). If they fail to do this, screw the Bowden control adjuster E in or out until neutral is obtained. Now release the clutch lever and the gear sliding fork should then enter the slot marked N, thus " centering " itself. When this is done re-tighten the pinch screw D.

WHEELS.

The bearings are packed with grease during assembly which will last until the machine is in need of a complete overhaul.

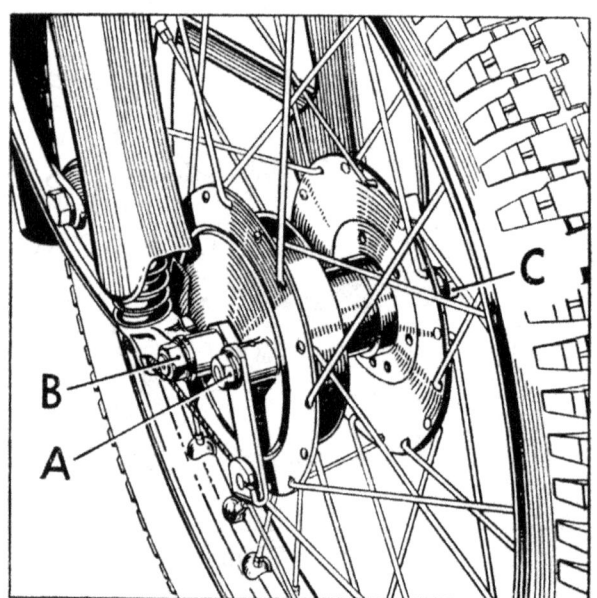

Fig. 26.   Front Wheel Removal.

Front Wheel Removal. To remove the front wheel from the forks, the brake cam spindle should be uncoupled by unscrewing the nut A, Fig. 26. The cam spindle is held on a square and careful note should be made of its position on this square for re-assembly. If a speedometer is fitted disconnect the cable from the speedometer gearbox. Take off the spindle nut B, and withdraw the wheel spindle C. As the spindle is withdrawn support the weight of the wheel; with the spindle withdrawn the wheel can be taken out sideways away from the brake anchor pin.

Rear Wheel Removal and Replacement. To remove the rear wheel, place the machine on its stand. Slacken the lower bolt A, Fig. 19, to free the brake anchor strap. Screw the chain adjusters F in as far as they will go. Unscrew the nuts B and withdraw the wheel spindle C. Move the wheel forward as far as it will go and disconnect the chain from the wheel sprocket. The wheel can then be withdrawn by either lifting the rear of the machine, or by leaning it over.

Re-assembly is carried out in the reverse order, but it is essential that the two distance pieces are replaced in their correct positions, i.e. the large one on the right hand side of the machine.

Wheel Bearings. The bearings are correctly adjusted when there is just perceptible side play (about 1/64 in.) detectable at the wheel rim. If the bearings require adjustment, slacken the wheel spindle Nut A, Figs. 27 and 28. Rotate the knurled adjusting ring B, turning in a clockwise direction to take up any slack. Then, gripping the knurled ring B firmly, re-tighten the spindle nut A and re-check the adjustment. (*Note* : In the case of the rear wheel, adjustment is preferably carried with the wheel removed.)

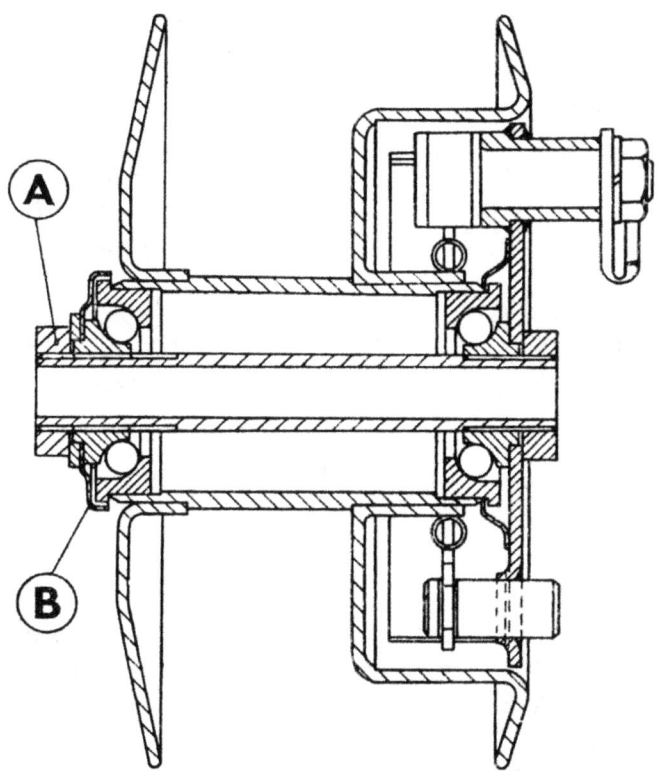

Fig. 27. Front Hub Arrangement.

Driving Chain Adjustment. The chain is adjusted with the machine on its stand. Rotate the wheel slowly until the tightest point in the chain is found, then check its up and down movement in the centre of the chain run. The total movement should be $\frac{3}{4}$ **inch** and if it varies from this setting then the chain must be adjusted by moving the rear wheel. Unscrew the wheel spindle nuts B, Fig. 19, slightly, and screw the adjusters F in or out as the case may be until the chain tension is correct.

Wheel Alignment. It is advisable to check the wheel alignment whenever the chain is adjusted, or the rear wheel is removed from the frame. The wheel alignment can be checked by glancing along the lines of both wheels when the front wheel is set straight, or by means of a long straight edge placed along the sides of the wheels. With the front wheel set straight ahead, the straight edge should touch both wheels.

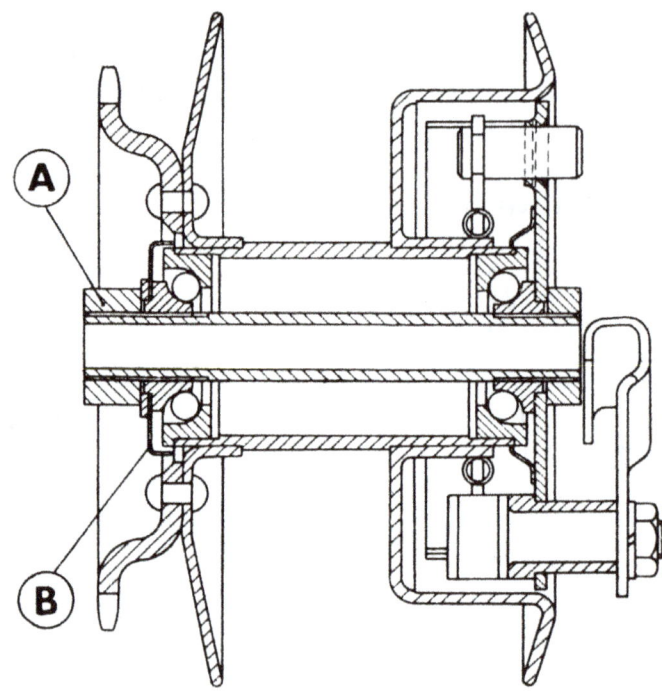

Fig. 28. Rear Hub Arrangement.

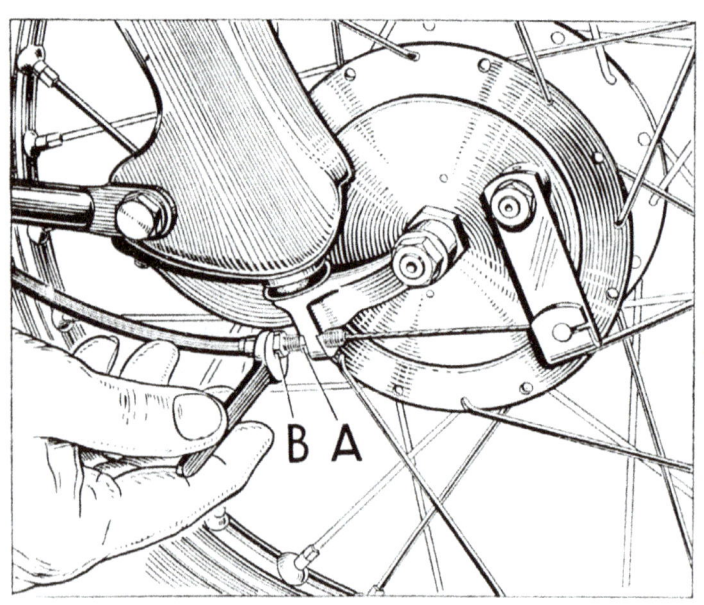

Fig. 29. Front Brake Adjustment.

Brakes. In the case of the rear brake, a knurled nut on the brake rod effects any adjustment necessary, and a few turns are all that is required to improve braking efficiency. The front brake is adjusted by means of the screwed cable stop at the lower end of the forks. Release locknut A and turn the adjuster B as shewn in Fig. 29.

FRAME AND FORKS.

Forks. There is no adjustment for the leading link type forks fitted to this machine. The only maintenance required is regular lubrication of the fork springs through the grease nipples attached to each fork as indicated on page 9.

Steering Head Adjustment. It is first necessary to raise the front wheel clear of the ground — this can best be done by lifting the machine on its stand and putting some small weight on the saddle or carrier causing the rear wheel to rest on the ground. Test for play by grasping the handlebars as shown in Fig. 16 and attempt to rock them up and down. If play can be detected, the head bearing requires adjusting. Release the hexagon A, Fig. 30, on top of the handlebar, slightly. Slacken the locknut B, and turn the adjusting nut C which is underneath, until any slackness has been taken up. Do not overtighten or the steering will be stiff and the ball races may be damaged. Re-tighten the locknut, and finally tighten the hexagon on top of the handlebar, taking care to re-set the handlebar alignment correctly.

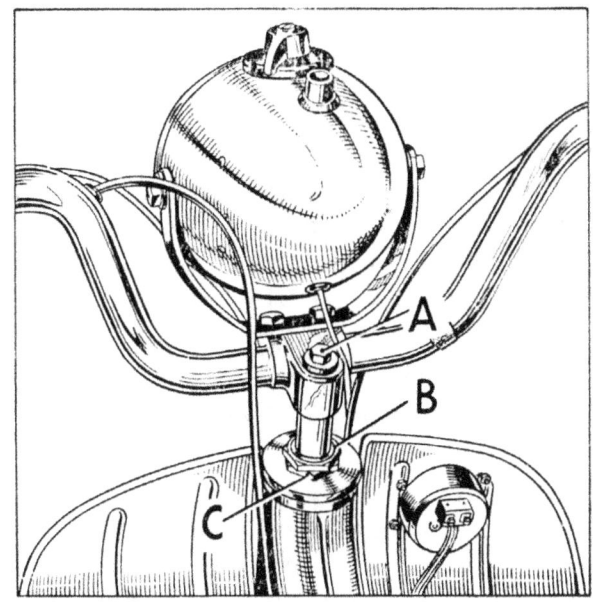

Fig. 30. Steering Head Adjustment.

Frame. The frame will not require any attention unless the machine has been involved in an accident. It should then be inspected very carefully and the wheel alignment checked. If the frame is damaged or distorted it must be replaced or returned to your B.S.A. dealer for rectification if feasible. The rear fork silentbloc type bushes have an extremely long life and the need for replacement is unlikely.

THE ELECTRICAL SYSTEM.

To gain access to the ignition system the engine must first be removed from the frame as explained on page 17. The equipment consists of a permanent magnet alternator which supplies direct lighting.

Generator. The flywheel comprises eight high grade cast magnets with pole pieces. It is **self-keeping** and may be separated from the stator without loss of magnetism. The laminated stator has seven salient poles, two of which are wound with coils of enamelled copper wire for the lighting circuit, and one for the ignition.

The set requires very little maintenance, and if the following notes are observed the life of the machine should prove trouble-free. Check, and if necessary, re-adjust the contacts once every 5,000 miles (8,000 kilometres) as described on page 14.

At the same time clean the contacts by inserting a dry piece of paper between them and withdrawing while the contacts are in the closed position. Do not allow the engine to run with grease or petrol on the contacts or they will start to burn and blacken. If they do, lightly polish with a piece of smooth emery cloth.

Smear the cam lubricating pad with a little grease every 5,000 miles (8,000 kilometres). Do not run with a faulty or damaged high tension lead, and occasionally clean away mud and dirt from around the high tension insulator. If the unit requires any attention beyond the replacement of the contact points and condensor, it is recommended that the complete machine should be taken or despatched to an authorised Wico Service Station.

Contact Breaker and Stator Unit. To remove this, first bend back the tab washer and remove the nut. The clutch driving cup and the flywheel can then be pulled off the mainshaft with the aid of an extractor, Part No. 61-3540. Remove the two screws A, Fig. 18 holding the stator. The whole unit can then be withdrawn, but care must be taken to ensure that the H.T. cable is pulled through the outer casing without any damage being sustained to it.

Electric Horn. The horn is adjusted at the factory to give its best performance and will give a long period of service without any attention. If it becomes uncertain in action, giving only a choking sound, or does not vibrate, it does not follow that it has broken down. First ascertain that the trouble is not due to some outside source such as a loose connection, or a short circuit in the wiring. If none of the above suggestions prove successful, the horn may be re-adjusted as follows :

Slacken the locknut on the front of the horn. A slight turn of the screw in or out while depressing the horn button with the engine running, will enable the best note to be obtained. Finally, re-tighten the locknut. If the horn still gives trouble, it should be taken to a Lucas Service Agent, or removed and returned to the manufacturers for rectification.

Headlamp. The lamp front, together with the reflector and bulb assembly, is secured to the main lamp assembly by means of a clip under the lamp. To replace a bulb or battery therefore, it is only necessary to loosen the clip and the rim can be removed.

The best way of checking the setting of the lamp is to stand the scooter in front of a light coloured wall at a distance of about 25 feet. If necessary, slacken the bolts securing the headlamp and move the lamp until, with the main driving light switched on, the beam is projected straight ahead and parallel with the ground. With the lamp in this position, the height of the beam centre on the wall should be the same as the height of the centre of the headlamp from the ground.

Rear Lamp. Twin bulbs are employed, one for use when the scooter is stationary and the current is being drawn from the battery, the other being used when the scooter's engine is running, drawing its current direct from the generator. The transparent red plastic portion of the lamp can be removed by unscrewing the countersunk screws.

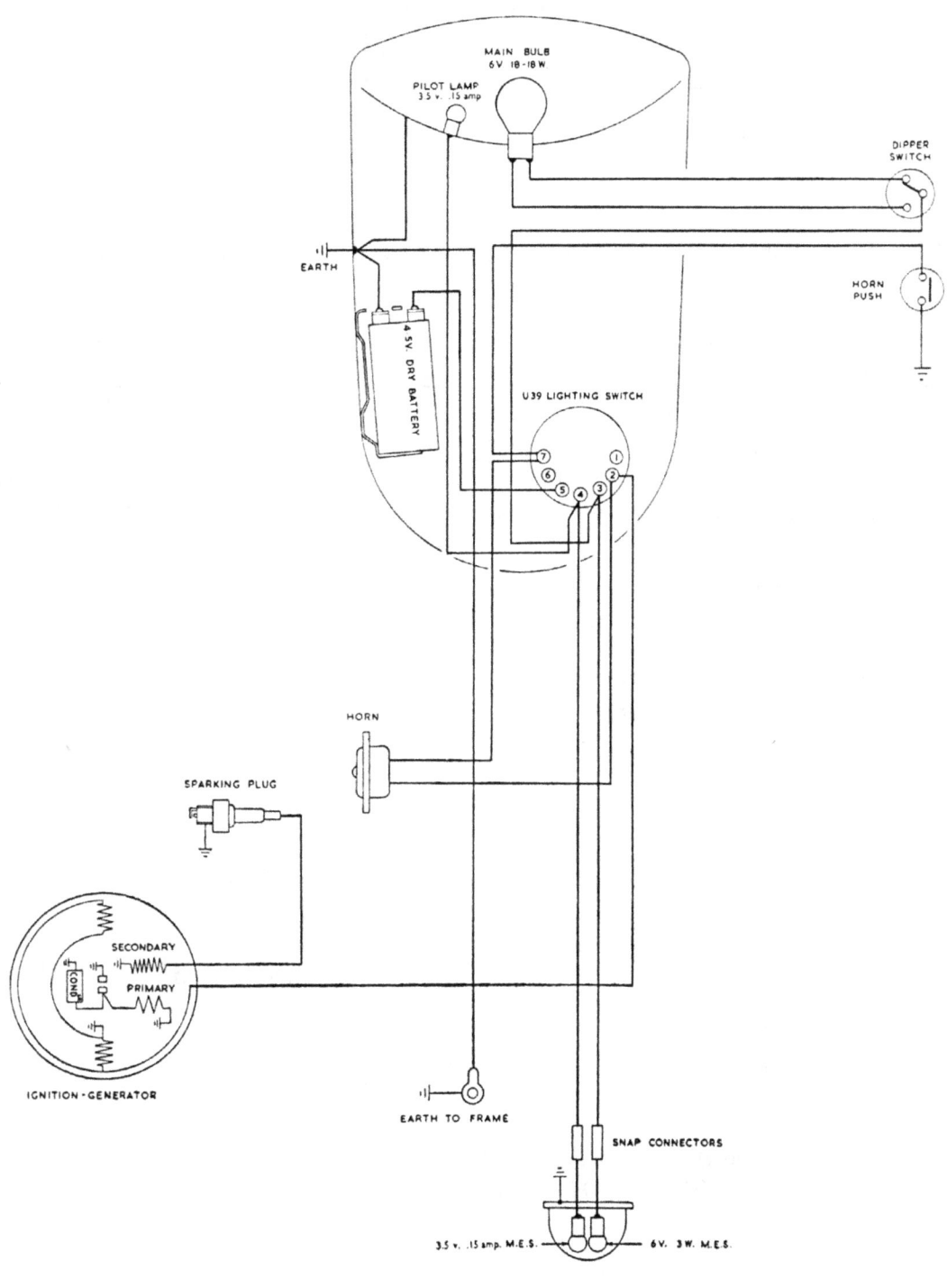

Fig. 31. Wiring Diagram.

GENERAL NOTES.

The wiring is connected by means of snap connectors at various convenient places on the machine and it is desirable occasionally to check it over and make certain that these connections are tight.

BULB TYPES.

Headlamp (main bulb) 6 v. 18/18 w.
Headlamp (pilot bulb) 3·5 v. 0·15 amp.
Rear lamp bulb 3·5 v. 0·15 amp. parking.
 6 v. ·05 amp. driving.

PROPRIETARY INSTRUMENTS, FITTINGS AND ACCESSORIES.

No expense is spared to secure as standard equipment the most suitable and highest quality instruments and accessories. Nevertheless, the Company's guarantee does not cover such parts, and in the event of trouble being experienced the parts in question should be returned to and claims made direct on the actual manufacturers, who will deal with them on the terms of their respective guarantees, as follows:

Carburetter:
Amal Ltd., Holford Works, Perry Barr, Birmingham.

Electrical Equipment:
Joseph Lucas Ltd., Birmingham.
Wico-Pacy Sales Corporation, Bletchley, Bucks.

Horn:
Joseph Lucas Ltd., Birmingham.
Clear Hooter Ltd., 33 Hampton Street, Birmingham.

Speedometer (if fitted):
Smith's Motor Accessories Ltd., Cricklewood, London N.W.2.

Tyres:
Dunlop Rubber Co. Ltd., Fort Dunlop, Birmingham.

Saddle:
Metal and Plastic Compacts Ltd., Montgomery Street, Sparkbrook, Birmingham.

SPECIAL NOTE

Prompt attention to all claims under guarantee will be ensured if your covering letter gives:
(1) Make, year and model, Engine and Frame No.
(2) Date of purchase and name of dealer from whom obtained.

TECHNICAL DATA.

Petrol tank capacity	6 pints
Bore	45 mm.
Stroke	44 mm.
Capacity	69·9 c.c.
Compression ratio	7·25—1
Piston ring gap — min.	·009"
max.	·013"
Piston ring side clearance	·002"
Contact breaker gap	·018"
Ignition timing: (piston distance before t.d.c. points just opening)	$\frac{5}{32}$"
Sparking plug — Champion	L10S
Plug points gap — min.	·018"
max.	·020"
Gear ratios — top	9·7
first	21·2
Wheel rims	G5-J
Tyre sizes	20–2$\frac{1}{2}$"
Tyre pressures* — front	18
rear	24
Chain size: $\frac{1}{2}$" x $\frac{3}{16}$" — pitches	70
Teeth on:	
rear chainwheel	27
gearbox sprocket	13
Total front wheel movement	2$\frac{1}{2}$"
Total rear wheel movement	2$\frac{1}{2}$"
Brake dimensions	4" x $\frac{7}{8}$"
Carburetter:	
bore	$\frac{1}{2}$"
main jet	35cc
throttle valve	3
needle position	3
needle jet	·0745"
Air cleaner	Amal

*The recommended tyre pressures are based on a rider's weight of 140 lb. If the rider is heavier increase the tyre pressures as follows:—

Front: Add 2 lb. per sq. in. for every 14 lb. increase above 140 lb.
Rear: Add 4 lb. per sq. in. for every 14 lb. increase above 140 lb.

If additional load is carried the actual load bearing upon each tyre should be determined and the pressures increased in accordance with the Dunlop Load and Pressure Schedule.

B.S.A. MOTOR CYCLES LTD., BIRMINGHAM 11

Telephones : Birmingham VICtoria 2381 (6 lines)
Telegrams and Cables : "SELMOTO", Birmingham

Service, Spares and Repairs Department—

Telephones : Birmingham VICtoria 2234 (30 lines)
Telegrams and Cables : "SELSERV", Birmingham

B.S.A. Motor Cycles Ltd., reserve the right to alter the designs or any constructional details of their manufacture at any time without giving notice.

MC.901-3   *Printed in England.*   Oct. 1956

BSA SPARES
DANDY 70 C.C.

Catalogue No. 00-5072

SUFFIX NUMBERS TO BE USED TO IDENTIFY VARYING FINISHES

/001 Cadmium
/003 Bright Chrome
/007 Black Enamel
/034 Devon Red
/084 Dark Lavender Grey
/085 Honey Beige
/104 Ivory
/128 Chrome Rim with Honey Beige Hub
/129 Chrome Rim with Dark Lavender Grey Hub
/130 Chrome Rim with Devon Red Hub

When ordering components with varying finishes, i.e., Petrol Tanks, Wheels, Rims, etc.—please state finish required by adding the appropriate number to part number.

EXAMPLE.

Petrol Tank, Dark Lavender Grey 64-8026/084.

INDEX, GRUPPEVERZEICHNIS, INDICE

				PAGE
Cylinder Cylinder Head Silencer	Cylindre Culasse Silencieux	Zylinder Zylinderkopf Auspufftopf	Cilindro Culata Silenciador	4
Engine	Moteur	Motor	Motor	6
Gearbox Chainguard	Boîte de vitesses Carter de chaîne	Getriebe Kettenkasten	Caja de velocidades Guardacadena	8
Gear Cluster Starter Pedal	Jeu d'engrenages Pedale de kick	Zahnradsatz Startkurbel	Juego de engranajes Arrancador	10
Frame	Cadre	Rahmen	Cuadro	12
Brake Pedal Stand Footrests	Pedale de frein Beguille Repose-pied	Fuss Bremshebel Ständer Fussrast	Pedal de freno Soporte Estribo	14
Front Fork	Fourche av	Vordergabel	Horquilla delantera	16
Front Wheel	Roue av	Vorderrad	Rueda delantera	18
Rear Wheel	Roue ar	Hinterrad	Rueda trasera	20
Saddle Petrol Tank Carrier	Selle Reservoir à carburant Porte-bagages	Sattel Kraftstoffbehalter Gepäckträger	Sillin Deposito de combustible Porta equipaje	22
Handlebar and Controls	Guidon et Commandes	Lenker und Steuerung	Manillar y Mandos	24
Legshields and Mudguards	Protège-jambes et Gardeboue	Beinschild und Schutzbleche	Guardapiernas y Guardabarros	26
Tools	Outils	Werkzeuger	Herramientos	28
Electrical and Sundries	Equipement electrique et Pièce variées	Elektr Ausrüstung und Sonstige Teile	Equip electrico y Piezas varias	30

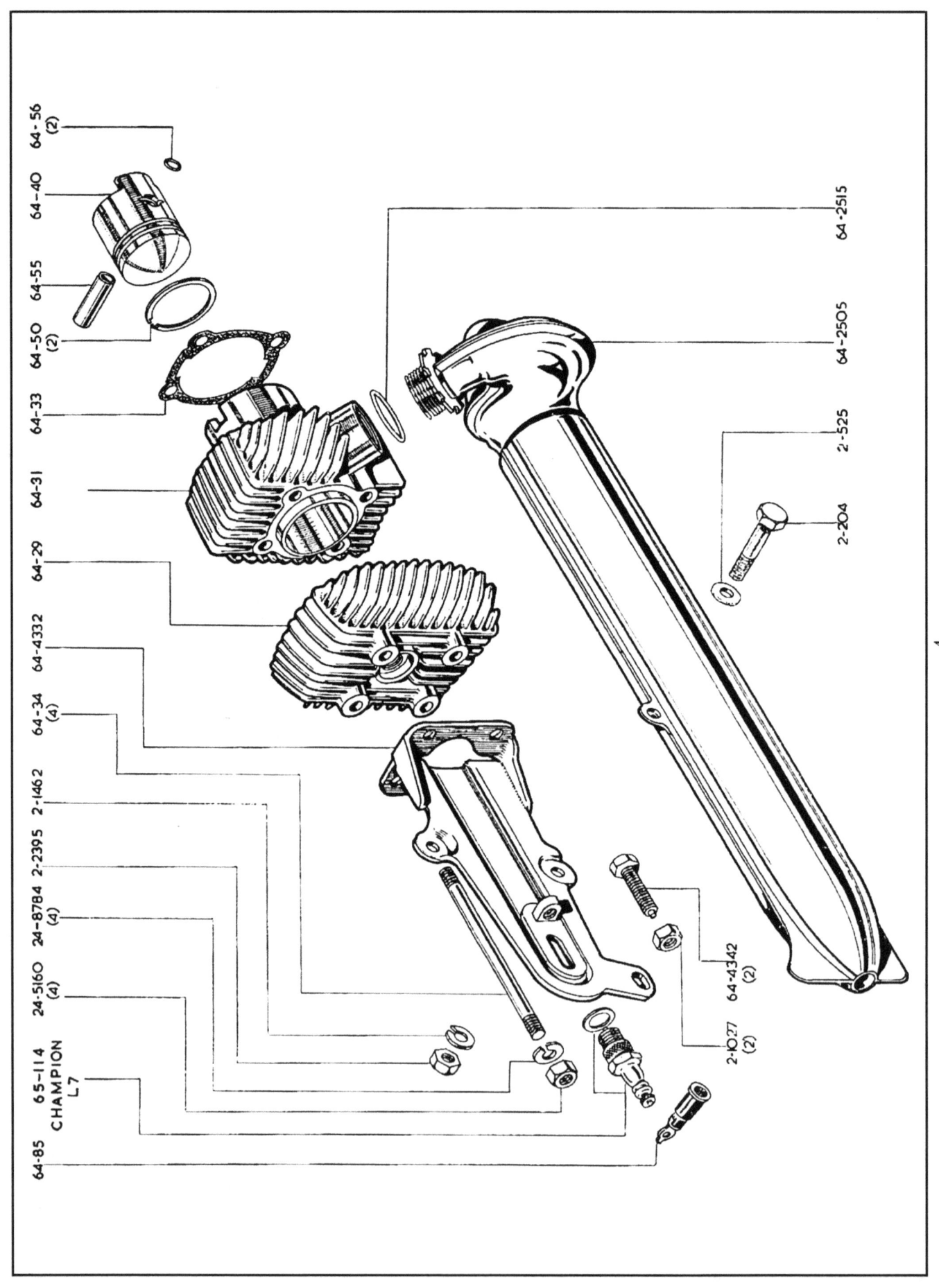

CYLINDER, CYLINDER HEAD, SILENCER. CYLINDRE, CULASSE, SILENCIEUX
ZYLINDER, ZYLINDERKOPF, AUSPUFFTOPF. CILINDRO, CULATA, SILENCIADOR

Part No. Bestell-nr No. de commande No. de parte	Description	Designation	Benennung	Descripción	Per Set Anzahl Nombre Juego de
2-204	Bolt	Boulon	Schraube	Tornillo	
2-525	Washer	Rondelle	Scheibe	Arandela	
2-1027	Nut	Écrou	Mutter	Tuerca	2
2-1462	Lockwasher	Arrêtoir	Sicherung	Freno	
2-2395	Nut	Écrou	Mutter	Tuerca	4
24-5160	Nut	Écrou	Mutter	Tuerca	4
24-8784	Lockwasher	Arrêtoir	Sicherung	Freno	
64-27	Sealing Ring	Bague d'étanchéité	Dichtring	Arandela de reten	
64-29	Cylinder Head	Culasse	Zylinderkopf	Culata	
64-31	Cylinder	Cylindre	Zylinder	Cilindro	
64-33	Gasket	Joint	Dichtung	Empaquetadura	
64-34	Stud	Goujon	Stehbolzen	Espárago	4
64-40	Piston Complete	Piston complète	Kolben Vollst	Embolo comp.	
64-43	Piston Complete + .015"	Piston complète + .39 mm.	Kolben Vollst + .39 mm.	Embolo comp. + .39 mm.	
64-45	Piston Complete + .030"	Piston complète + .79 mm.	Kolben Vollst + .79 mm.	Embolo comp. + .79 mm.	
64-50	Piston Ring	Segment	Verdichtungsring	Segmento	2
64-51	Piston Ring + .015"	Segment + .39 mm.	Verdichtungsring + .39 mm.	Segmento + .39 mm.	2
64-52	Piston Ring + .030"	Segment + .79 mm.	Verdichtungsring + .79 mm.	Segmento + .79 mm.	2
64-55	Gudgeon Pin	Axe de piston	Kolbenbolzen	Bulón de embolo	
64-56	Circlip	Arrêtoir	Sicherung	Freno	2
64-85	Ignition Lead Terminal	Borne de cable d'allumage	Zündleitungsstecker	Borne de conexión	
64-114	Spark Plug	Bougie d'allumage	Zündkerze	Bujía	
64-2505	Silencer	Silencieux	Auspufftopf	Silenciador	
64-2515	Sealing Ring	Bague d'étanchéité	Dichtring	Arandela de reten	
64-4332	Blade R/H	Lame (droite)	Blatt (Rechts)	Hoja (derecha)	2
64-4342	Bolt	Boulon	Schraube	Tornillo	

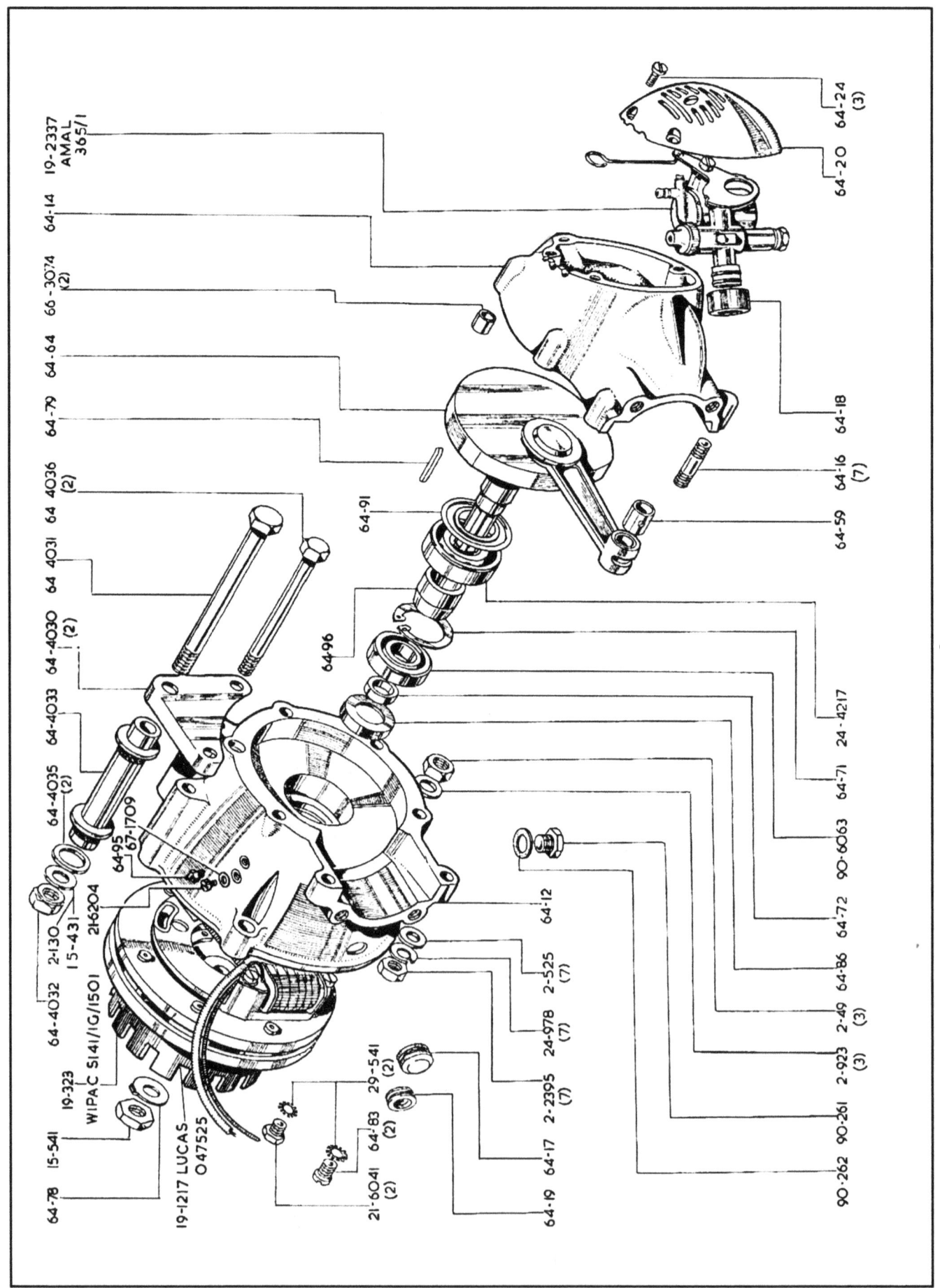

ENGINE. MOTEUR. MOTOR. MOTOR

Part No. No. de commande Bestell-nr No. de parte	Description	Designation	Benennung	Descripción	Per Set Nombre Anzahl Juego de
2-49	Nut	Ecrou	Mutter	Tuerca	3
2-130	Washer	Rondelle	Scheibe	Arandela	7
2-525	Washer	Rondelle	Scheibe	Arandela	3
2-923	Washer	Rondelle	Scheibe	Arandela	7
2-2395	Nut	Ecrou	Mutter	Tuerca	
15-431	Washer	Rondelle	Scheibe	Arandela	
15-541	Nut	Ecrou	Mutter	Tuerca	
19-323	Generator (Wico Pacy)	Générateur (Wico Pacy)	Generator (Wico Pacy)	Generador (Wico Pacy)	
19-1217	Generator (Lucas)	Générateur (Lucas)	Generator (Lucas)	Generador (Lucas)	
19-2337	Carburetter	Carburateur	Vergaser	Carburador	
21-6041	Bolt	Boulon	Schraube	Tornillo	2
24-978	Lockwasher	Arrêtoir	Sicherung	Freno	7
24-4217	Bearing	Roulement	Lager	Rolamiento	
29-541	Lockwasher	Arrêtoir	Sicherung	Freno	2
*64-12	Crankcase L/H	Carter de vilebrequin-gauche	Kurbelgehäuse-Links	Caja de cigüeñal-izq	
*64-14	Crankcase R/H	Carter de vilebrequin-droite	Kurbelgehäuse-Rechts	Caja de cigüeñal-der	
64-16	Stud	Goujon	Stehbolzen	Esparago	7
64-17	Rubber Plug	Cale caoutchouc	Gummistopfen	Tapón de goma	
64-18	Plastic Sleeve	Manchon plastique	Kunststoffhülse	Manguito plastico	
64-19	Rubber Grommet	Manchon caoutchouc	Gummitülle	Manguera de goma	
64-20	Cover	Chapeau de protection	Schutzkappe	Tapa	
64-24	Screw	Vis	Schraube	Tornillo	3
64 59	Bush	Douille	Büchse	Casquillo	
64 64	Crankshaft Assembly	Embiellage	Kurbeltrieb	Cigüeñal	
64-71	Circlip	Arrêtoir	Sicherung	Freno	
64-72	Oil Seal Ring	Joint d'huile	Öldichtung	Reten de aceite	2
64-78	Lockwasher	Arrêtoir	Sicherung	Freno	
64-79	Cotter	Clavette à rainure	Nutenkeil	Chaveta ordinaria	
64-83	Screw	Vis	Schraube	Tornillo	2
64-86	Oil Seal	Joint d'huile	Dichtring	Reten de aceite	
64-94	Grease Tube	Tube à graisse	Schmierrohr	Tubo de grasa	2
64-95	Grease Nipple	Graisseur	Schmiernippel	Engrasador	
64-96	Spacer Bush	Bague d'écartement	Distanzring	Anillo espaciador	
64-3074	Dowel	Goupille cylindrique	Stift	Pasador	2
64-4030	Engine Plate	Plaque d'appui pour moteur	Motorabstützblech	Placa de apoyo del motor	
64-4031	Pivot Bolt	Boulon	Schraube	Tornillo	
64-4032	Self Locking Nut	Ecrou d'arrêt	Selbstsicherungsmutter	Tuerca de seguridad	
64-4033	Spacer Tube	Tube entretoise	Abstandrohr	Tubo espaciador	
64-4035	Washer	Rondelle	Scheibe	Arandela	
64-4036	Bolt	Boulon	Schraube	Tornillo	
67-1709	Washer	Rondelle	Scheibe	Arandela	2
90-261	Drain Plug	Bouchon de vidange d'huile	Ablass Schraube	Tapón	2
90-262	Sealing Ring	Bague d'étanchéïté	Dichtring	Junta	2
90 6063	Bearing	Roulement	Lager	Rolamiento	

*Supplied only as crankcase complete 64-11.
*Livrés seulement comme carter complet 64-11.

*Nur Auss Collvollständige Gehäuse Geliefert 64-11.
*Suministrads solamente como carter completo 64-11.

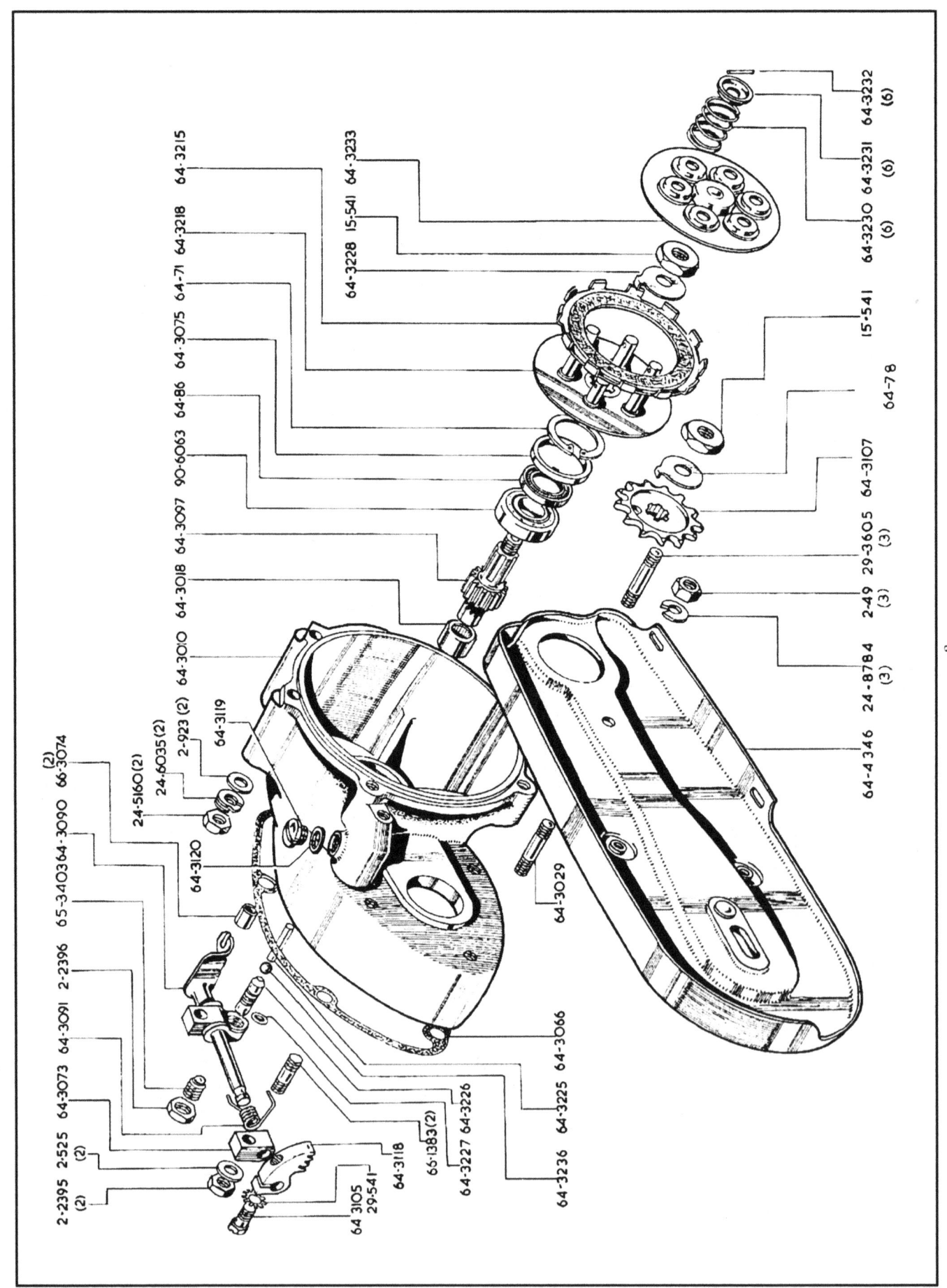

GEARBOX, CHAINGUARD. BOITE de VITESSES, CARTER de CHAINE GETRIEBE, KETTENKASTEN. CAJA de VELOCIDADES, GUARDACADENA

Part No. / No. de commande / Bestell-nr / No. de parte	Description	Designation	Benennung	Descripción	Per Set / Nombre / Anzahl / Juego de
2-49	Nut	Ecrou	Mutter	Tuerca	3
2-525	Washer	Rondelle	Scheibe	Arandela	2
2-923	Washer	Rondelle	Scheibe	Arandela	2
2-2395	Nut	Ecrou	Mutter	Tuerca	2
2-2396	Nut	Ecrou	Mutter	Tuerca	
15-541	Nut	Ecrou	Mutter	Tuerca	2
24-6035	Lockwasher	Arrêtoir	Sicherung	Freno	2
24-8784	Lockwasher	Arrêtoir	Sicherung	Freno	2
29-541	Lockwasher	Arrêtoir	Sicherung	Freno	3
29-3605	Stud	Goujon	Stehbolzen	Esparago	
64-71	Circlip	Arrêtoir	Sicherung	Freno	3
64-78	Lockwasher	Arrêtoir	Sicherung	Freno	
64-86	Oil Seal	Joint d'huile	Dichtring	Reten de aceite	
64-3010	Gearbox Case	Carter de changement de vitesses.	Getriebegehäuse	Caja de velocidades	
64-3018	Bearing	Roulement	Lager	Rolamiento	
64-3029	Stud	Goujon	Stehbolzen	Esparago	
64-3066	Gasket	Joint	Dichtung	Empaquetadura	
64-3073	Bearing Block	Palier	Lager	Cojinete	
64-3075	Oil Seal Ring	Bague du joint d'huile	Dichtring	Anillo del reten de aceite	
64-3090	Gearchange Spindle	Arbre de commande de changement de vitesses.	Schaltwelle	Arbol de cambio	
64-3091	Spring	Ressort	Feder	Resorte	
64-3097	Drive Shaft	Arbre d'entraînement	Antreibswelle	Arbol de transmisión	
64-3105	Bolt	Boulon	Schraube	Tornillo	
64-3107	Sprocket	Pignon	Ritzel	Piñon	
64-3118	Locking Arm	Levier d'arrêt	Sperrhebel	Brazo trabador	
64-3119	Plug	Bouzon	Schraube	Tornillo	
64-3120	Sealing Washer	Joint	Dichtung	Arandela de reten	
64-3215	Driving Plate	Disque d'entraînement	Mitnehmerplatte	Placa de manda	
64-3218	Clutch Back Plate	Plateau d'embrayage	Kupplungsscheibe	Placa del embrague	
64-3225	Clutch Rod (long)	Tige de traction (longue)	Zugstange (Lang)	Varilla del embrague (larga)	
64-3226	Clutch Rod (short)	Tige de traction (courte)	Zugstange (Kurz)	Varilla del embrague (corta)	
64-3227	"O" Ring	Bague "O"	"O" Ring	Anillo "O"	
64-3228	Lockwasher	Arrêtoir	Sicherung	Freno	
64-3230	Spring	Resort	Feder	Resorte	6
64-3231	Spring Cup	Douille	Hülse	Copa	6
64-3232	Peg	Goupille	Sicherungsstift	Esparago	6
64-3233	Clutch Pressure Plate	Disque extérieur d'embrayage	Äussere Kupplungsscheibe	Disco exterior del embrague	
64-3236	Ball	Bille	Kugel	Bola	
64-4346	Chainguard	Carter de chaîne	Kettenkasten	Guardacadena	
65-3403	Screw	Vis	Schraube	Tornillo	
66-1383	Stud	Goujon	Stehbolzen	Esparago	2
66-3074	Dowel	Goupille cylindrique	Stift	Pasador	2
90-6063	Bearing	Roulement	Lager	Rolamiento	

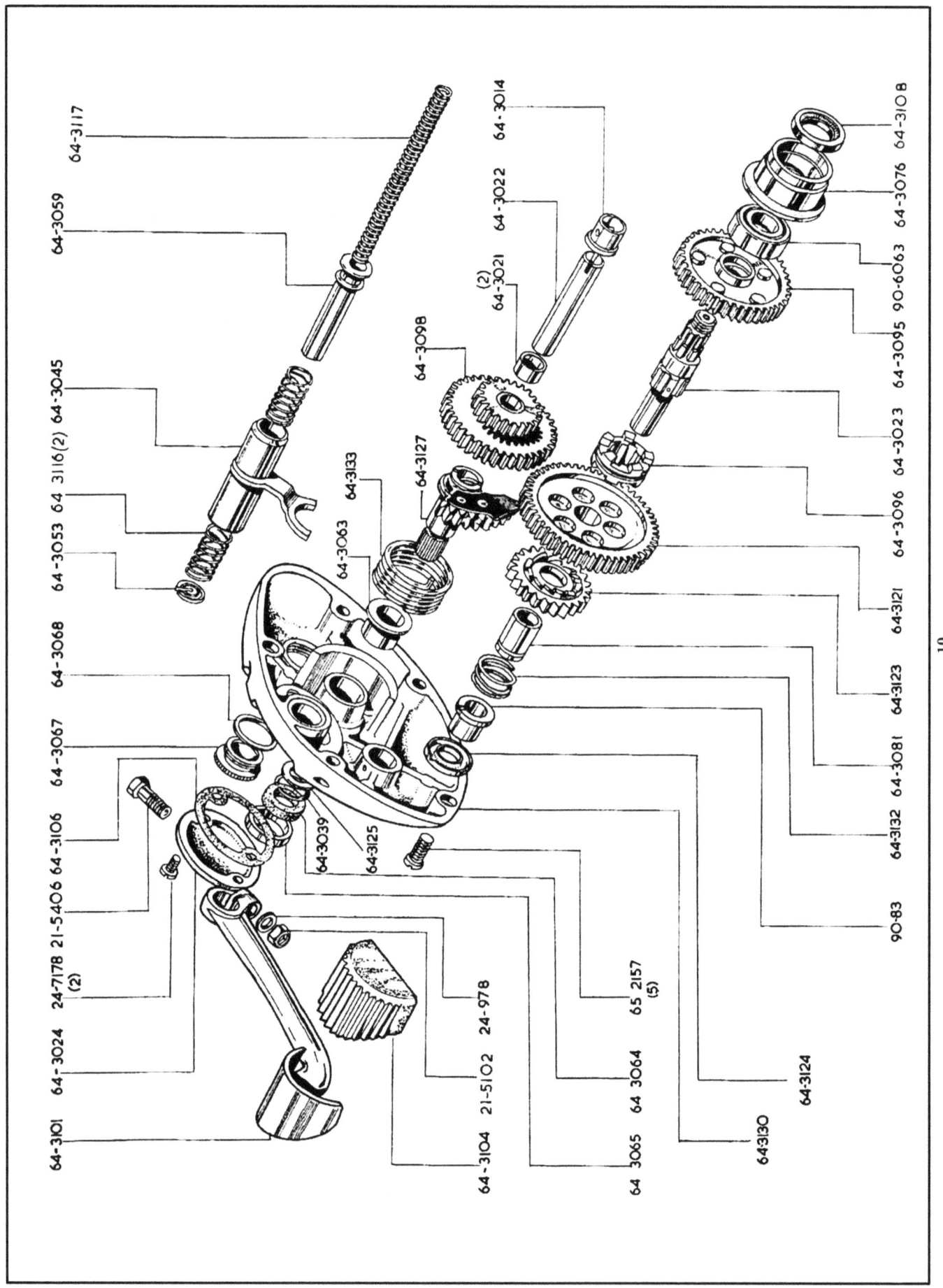

GEAR CLUSTER, STARTER PEDAL. JEU D'ENGRENAGES, PEDALE de KICK ZAHNRADSATZ. STARTKURBEL. JUEGO de ENGRANAJES, ARRANCADOR

Part No. / No. de commande / Bestell-nr / No. de parte	Description	Designation	Benennung	Descripción	Per Set / Nombre / Anzahl / Juego de
21-5102	Nut	Ecrou	Mutter	Tuerca	
21-5406	Bolt	Boulon	Schraube	Tornillo	
24-978	Washer	Rondelle	Scheibe	Arandela	
24-7178	Screw	Vis	Schraube	Tornillo	2
64-3014	Bush	Douille	Büchse	Casquillo	
64-3021	Bus	Douille	Büchse	Casquillo	2
64-3022	Axle	Axe	Achse	Eje	
64-3023	Shaft	Arbre	Welle	Arbol	
64-3024	Cover Plate	Couvercle de palier	Lagerdeckel	Tapa del cojinete	
64-3039	Circlip	Arrêtoir	Sicherung	Freno	
64-3045	Selector Fork	Fourchette de commande de changement de vitesses	Schaltgabel	Horquilla de mando de caja de velocidades	
64-3053	Anchor Plate	Support	Halter	Soporte	
64-3059	Spring Casing	Capuchon de resort	Federhülse	Manguito del resorte	
64-3063	Bush	Douille	Büchse	Casquillo	
64-3064	Felt Washer	Rondelle feutre	Filz Scheibe	Arandela de fieltro	
64-3065	Oil Seal	Joint d'huile	Dichtring	Reten de aceite	
64-3067	Cap	Rondelle chapeau	Abdeckkappe	Tapon	
64-3068	Gasket	Joint	Dichtung	Empaquetadura	
64-3076	Bearing Housing	Boîtier de palier	Lagergehäuse	Caja del cojinete	
64-3081	Bush	Douille	Büchse	Casquillo	
64-3095	Pinion 42T	Pignon D-	Zahnrad Z.-	Piñón D -	
64-3096	Sliding Dog	Crabot Coulissant	Schiereklaue	Garra deslizantento	
64-3098	Gear Cluster	Jeu d'engrenages	Zahnradsatz	Juego de engranajes	
64-3101	Starter Pedal	Pedale de kick	Startkurbel	Arrancador	
64-3104	Rubber Pad	Revêtement caoutchouc	Gummiauflage	Cojin de goma	
64-3106	Gasket	Joint	Dichtung	Empaquetadura	
64-3108	Oil Seal	Joint d'huile	Dichtring	Reten de aceite	
64-3116	Spring	Ressort	Feder	Resorte	2
64-3117	Spring	Ressort	Feder	Resorte	
64-3121	Pinion 53T	Pignon D-	Zahnrad Z.-	Piñón D	
64-3123	Ratchet Pinion	Pignon du rochet	Sperrwerkrad	Rueda de trinquete	
64-3124	Cup	Cuvette	Lagerchale	Grapa	
64-3125	Washer	Rondelle	Scheibe	Arandela	
64-3127	Quadrant	Secteur	Segment	Sector	
64-3130	Cover	Chapeau de protection	Schutzkappe	Tapa	
64-3132	Spring	Ressort	Feder	Resorte	
64-3133	Spring	Ressort	Feder	Resorte	
65-2157	Screw	Vis	Schraube	Tornillo	5
90-83	Bush	Douille	Büchse	Casquillo	
90-6063	Bearing	Roulement	Lager	Rolamiento	

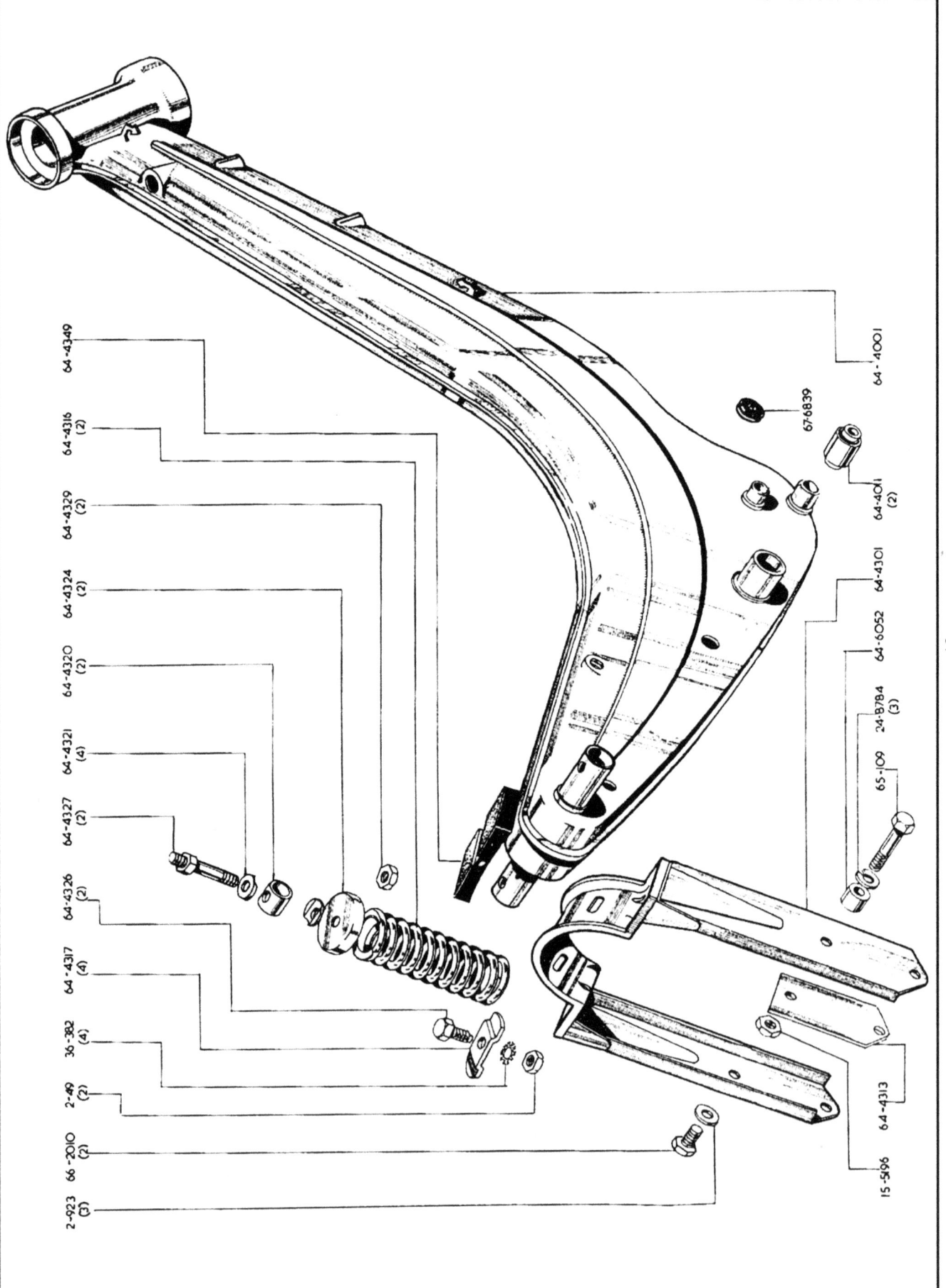

FRAME. CADRE. RAHMEN. CUADRO

Part No. No de commande Bestell-nr No. de parte	Description	Designation	Benennung	Descripción	Per Set Nombre Anzahl Juego de
2-49	Nut	Ecrou	Mutter	Tuerca	2
2-923	Washer	Rondelle	Scheibe	Arandela	3
15-5196	Nut	Ecrou	Mutter	Tuerca	
24-8784	Lockwasher	Arrêtoir	Sicherung	Freno	3
36-382	Lockwasher	Arrêtoir	Sicherung	Freno	4
64-4001	Frame	Cadre	Rahmen	Cuadro	
64-4011	Bush	Douille	Büchse	Casquillo	2
64-4301	Rear Fork	Fourche ar.	Hinterradgabel	Horquilla tras.	
64-4313	Plate	Plaque	Scheibe	Placa	
64-4316	Spring	Ressort	Feder	Resorte	2
64-4317	Spring Plate	Support	Halter	Sujeción	4
64-4320	Bush	Douille	Büchse	Casquillo	2
64-4321	Saddle Washer	Rondelle pour selle	Sattelscheibe	Arandela para silín	4
64-4324	Spring Cup	Douille	Hülse	Copa	2
64-4326	Bolt	Boulon	Schraube	Tornillo	2
64-4327	Stud	Goujon	Stehbolzen	Espátago	2
64-4329	Nut	Ecrou	Mutter	Tuerca	2
64-4349	Rubber Pad	Revêtement caoutchouc	Gummiauflage	Cojín de goma	2
64-6052	Spacer Tube	Tube entretoise	Abstandrohr	Tubo espaciador	
65-109	Bolt	Boulon	Schraube	Tornillo	
66-2010	Bolt	Boulon	Schraube	Tornillo	
67-6839	Rubber Grommet	Manchon caoutchouc	Gummitülle	Manguera de goma	2

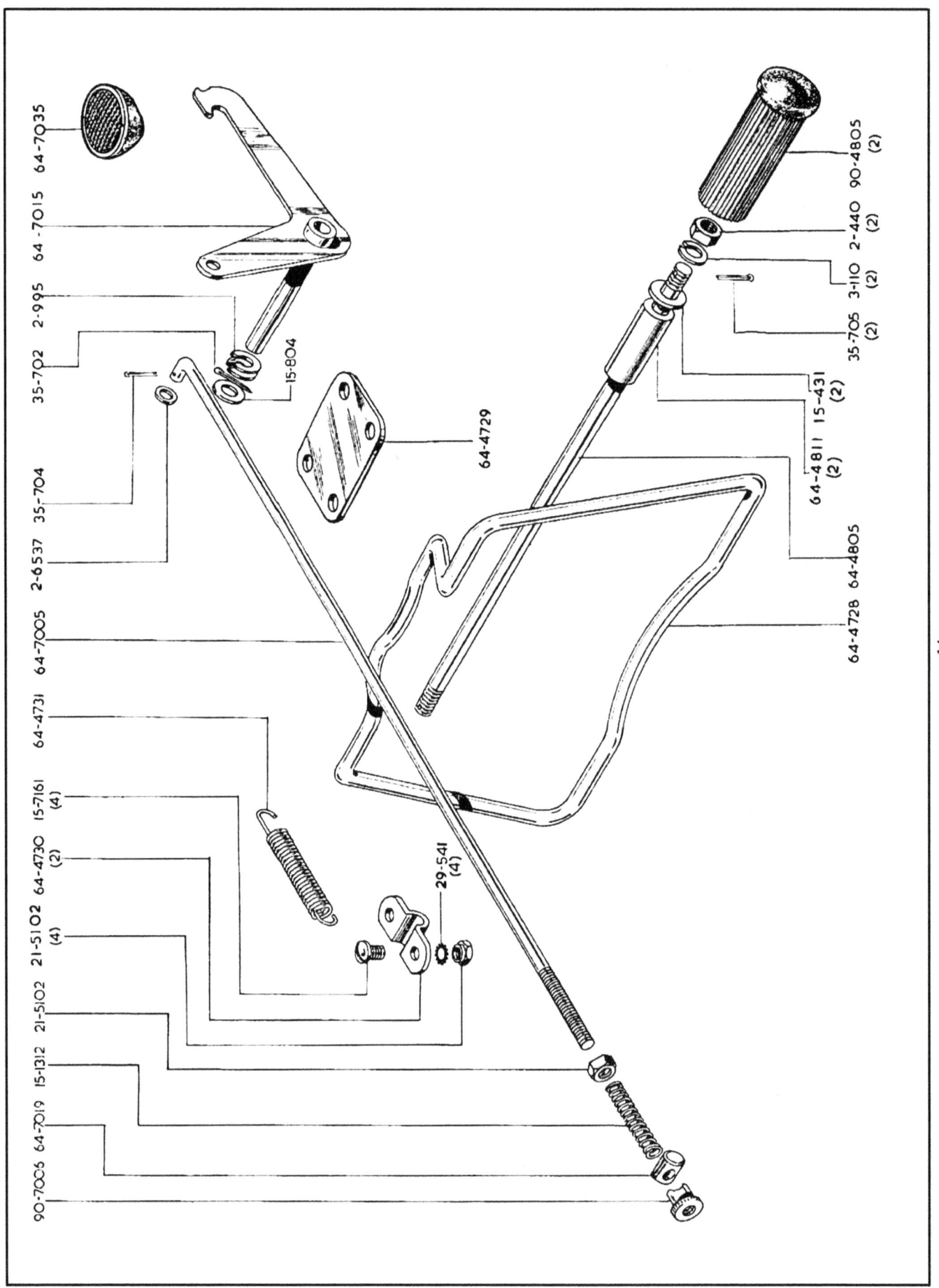

BRAKE PEDAL, STAND, FOOTRESTS. PEDALE de FREIN, BEQUILLE, REPOSE-PIED PEDALE de FRENO, SOPORTE, ESTRIBO
FUSSBREMSHEBEL, STANDER, FUSSRAST. PEDAL de FRENO, SOPORTE, ESTRIBO

Part No. No. de commande Bestell-nr No. de parte	Description	Designation	Benennung	Descripción	Per Set Nombre Anzahl Juego de
2-440	Nut	Ecrou	Mutter	Tuerca	2
2-995	Lockwasher	Arrêtoir	Sicherung	Freno	
2-6537	Washer	Rondelle	Scheibe	Arandela	2
3-110	Lockwasher	Arrêtoir	Sicherung	Freno	2
15-431	Washer	Rondelle	Scheibe	Arandela	
15-804	Washer	Rondelle	Scheibe	Arandela	
15-1312	Spring	Ressort	Feder	Resorte	4
15-7161	Screw	Vis	Schraube	Tornillo	5
21-5102	Nut	Ecrou	Mutter	Tuerca	1
29-541	Lockwasher	Arrêtoir	Sicherung	Freno	
35-702	Split Pin	Goupille	Splint	Chaveta hendida	2
35-704	Split Pin	Goupille	Splint	Chaventa hendida	
35-705	Split Pin	Goupille	Splint	Chaveta hendida	
64-4728	Stand	Bequille centrale	Kippstander	Soporte central	
64-4729	Plate	Plaque	Scheibe	Placa	2
64-4730	Bracket	Support	Lagerbock	Soporte	
64-4731	Spring	Ressort	Feder	Resorte	
64-4805	Footrest Rod	Tringle marchepied	Fußrettstange	Varilla del estribo	
64-4811	Spacer Tube	Tube entretoise	Abstandrohr	Tubo espaciador	2
64-7005	Brake Rod	Tringle de frein	Zugstange	Tirante de freno	
64-7015	Brake Pedal	Pédale de frein	Fussbremshebel	Pedal de freno	
64-7019	Swivel Pin	Goupille simple	Stift	Esparago	
64-7035	Rubber Pad	Revêtement caoutchouc	Gummiauflage	Cojin de goma	
90-4805	Rubber Pad	Revêtement caoutchouc	Gummiauflage	Cojin de goma	2
90-7006	Adjuster Nut	Ecrou de réglage	Verstellungsmutter	Tuerca de ajuste	

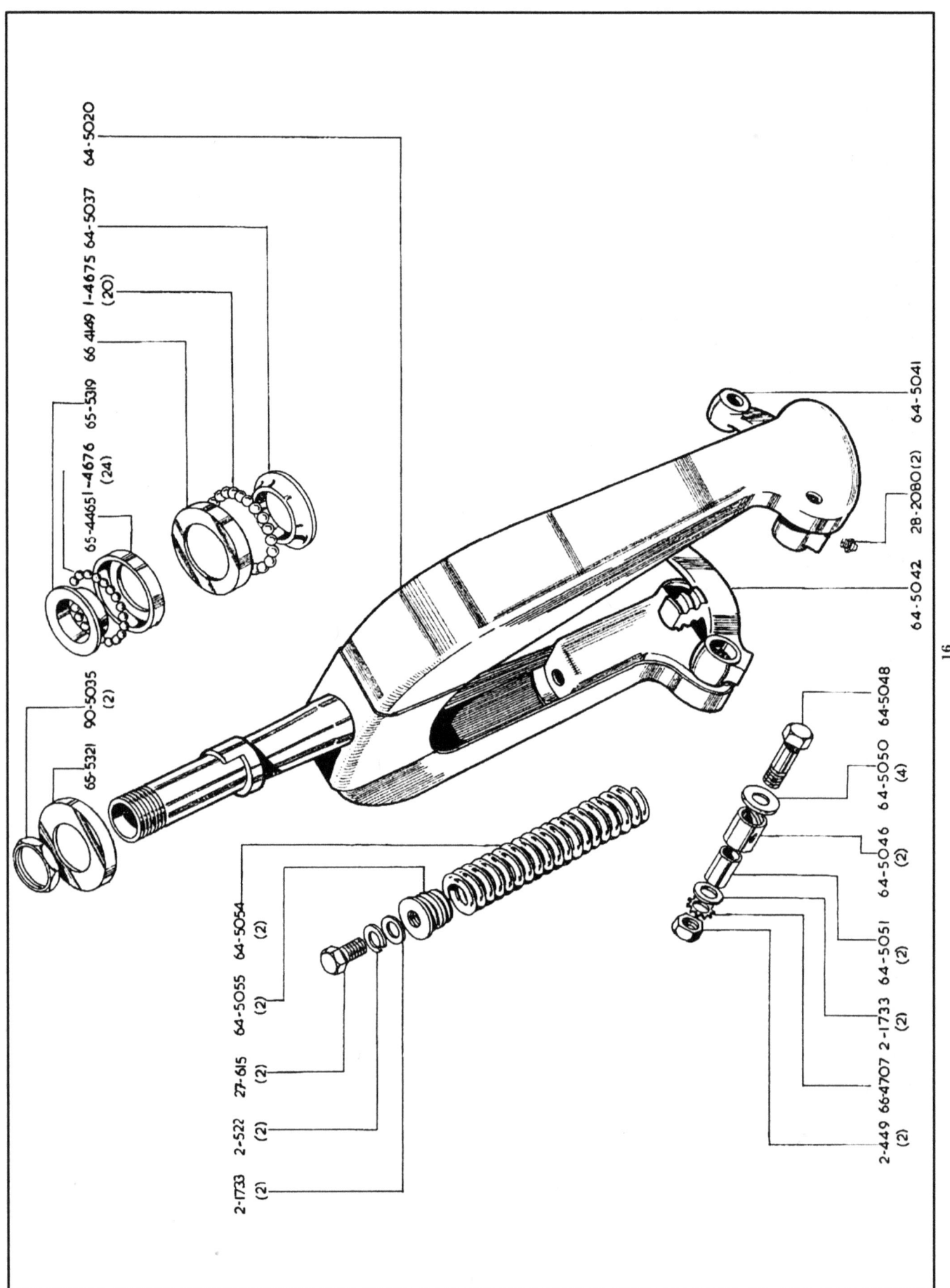

FRONT FORK. FOURCHE AV. VORDERGABEL. HORQUILLA DELANTERA

Part No. / No de commande / Bestell-nr / No. de parte	Description	Désignation	Benennung	Descripción	Per Set / Nombre / Anzahl / Juego de
1-4675	Ball (lower)	Bille (inférieure)	Kugel Unten	Bola inf.	20
1-4676	Ball (upper)	Bille (supérieure)	Kugel Oben	Bola sup.	24
2-449	Nut	Ecrou	Mutter	Tuerca	2
2-522	Lockwasher	Arrêtoir	Sicherung	Freno	2
2-1733	Washer	Rondelle	Scheibe	Arandela	4
27-615	Bolt	Boulon	Schraube	Tornillo	2
28-2080	Grease Nipple	Graisseur	Schmiernippel	Engrasador	2
64-5020	Front Fork Complete	Fourche avant complète	Vordergabel Vollst	Horquilla delantera comp.	
64-5037	Bearing Cone (lower)	Cône inférieure	Lagerkonus Unten	Cona de cojinete inf.	
64-5041	Pivot Link R/H	Biellette oscillante (droite)	Schwinghebel (Rechts)	Brida pivotante (der)	
64-5042	Pivot Link L/H	Biellette oscillante (gauche)	Schwinghebel (Links)	Brida pivotante (izq)	
64-5046	Bush	Douille	Büchse	Casquillo	2
64-5048	Bolt	Boulon	Schraube	Tornillo	
64-5050	Washer	Rondelle	Scheibe	Arandela	4
64-5051	Spacer Tube	Tube entretoise	Abstandrohr	Tubo espaciador	2
64-5054	Spring	Ressort	Feder	Resorte	2
64-5055	Spring Anchorage	Ancrage du ressort	Federanker	Sujeción del resorte	2
65-4465	Bearing Cup (upper)	Cuvette de roulement (sup.)	Lagerschale (Oben)	Copa de rolamiento (sup.)	
65-5319	Bearing Cone (upper)	Cône (supérieure)	Lagerkonus (Oben)	Cona de cojinete (sup.)	
65-5321	Cap	Rondelle chapeau	Abdeckkappe	Tapon	
66-4149	Bearing Cup (lower)	Cuvette de roulement (inf.)	Lagerschale (Unten)	Copa de rolamiento (inf.)	
66-4707	Lockwasher	Arrêtoir	Sicherung	Freno	
90-5035	Adjuster Nut	Ecrou de réglage	Verstellungsmutter	Tuerca de ajuste	2

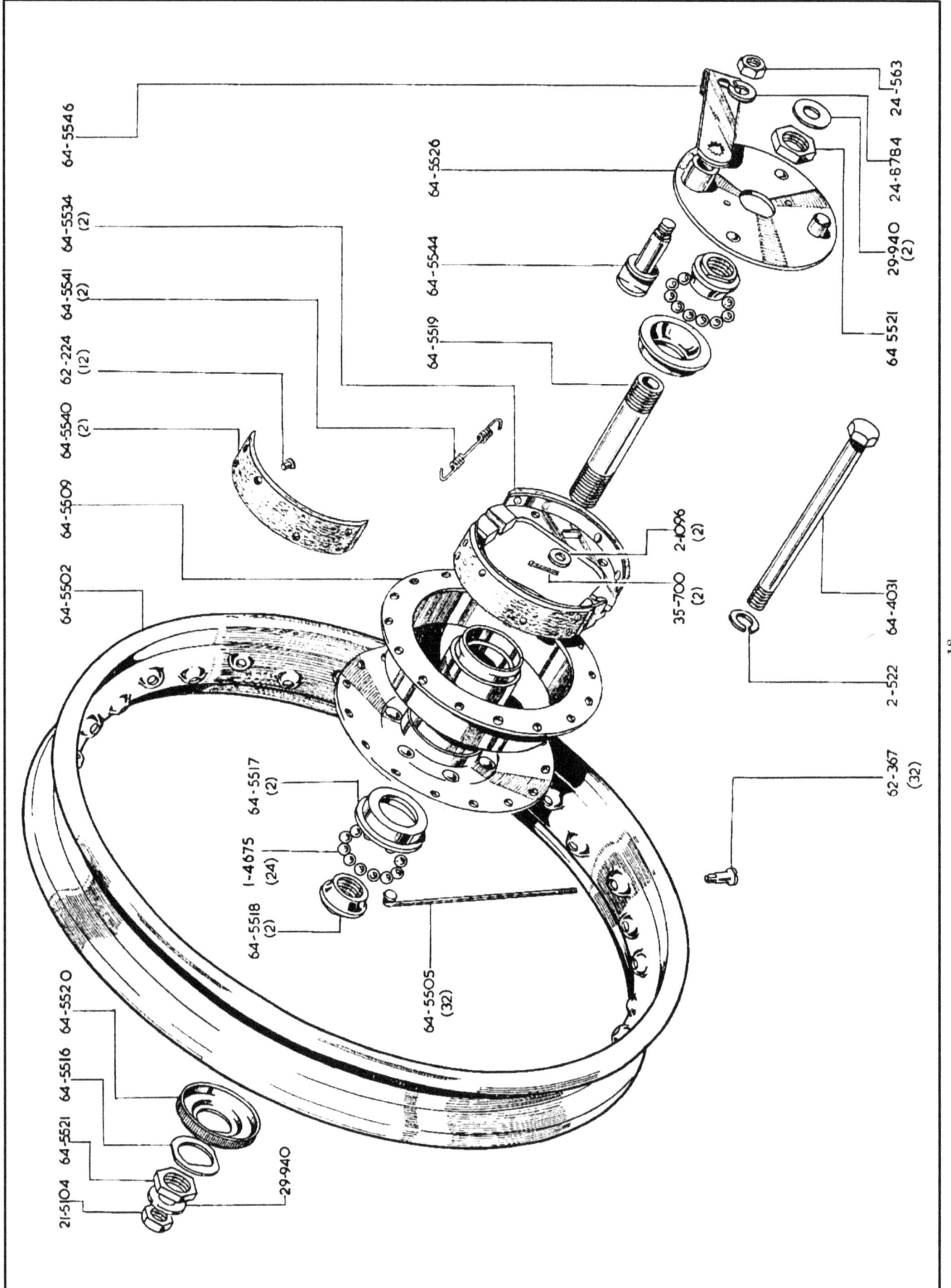

FRONT WHEEL. ROUE AV. VORDERRAD. RUEDA DALANTERA

Part No. / No. de commande / Bestell-nr / No. de parte	Description	Désignation	Benennung	Descripción	Per Set / Nombre / Anzahl / Juego de
1-4675	Ball	Bille	Kugel	Bola	24
2-522	Lockwasher	Arrêtoir	Sicherung	Freno	
2-1096	Washer	Rondelle	Scheibe	Arandela	2
21-5104	Nut	Ecrou	Mutter	Tuerca	
24-563	Nut	Ecrou	Mutter	Tuerca	
24-8784	Lockwasher	Arrêtoir	Sicherung	Freno	
*29-940	Washer	Rondelle	Scheibe	Arandela	3
35-700	Split Pin	Goupille	Splint	Chaveta hendida	2
62-224	Rivet	Rivet	Niet	Remache	2
62-367	Nipple	Ecrou	Nipple	Tuerca	32
64-4031	Axle	Axe	Achse	Eje	
64-5501	Front Wheel	Roue av.	Vorderrad	Rueda delantera	
64-5502	Rim	Jante	Felge	Llanta	
64-5505	Spoke	Rayon	Speiche	Raio	32
64-5509	Front Hub	Moyeu de roue av.	Vorderradnabe	Cubo de rueda del	
64-5516	Washer	Rondelle	Scheibe	Arandela	
64-5517	Bearing Cup	Cuvette de roulement	Lagerschale	Copa de rolamiento	
64-5518	Bearing Cone	Cone	Lagerkonus	Cona de cojinete	
64-5519	Spacer Tube	Tube entretoise	Abstandrohr	Tubo espaciador	
64-5520	Cap	Rondelle chapeau	Abdeckkappe	Tapon	
64-5521	Nut	Ecrou	Mutter	Tuerca	2
64-5526	Brake Back Plate	Disque de frein	Bremsscheibe	Disco de freno	
64-5534	Brake Shoe	Segment	Bremsbacke	Zapata	2
64-5540	Brake Lining	Garniture	Belag	Guarnición	2
64-5541	Spring	Ressort	Feder	Resorte	2
64-5544	Brake Cam	Clé de frein	Bremsschlüssel	Llave de freno	
64-5546	Brake Cam Lever	Levier de frein	Bremshebel	Palanca de freno	

*Four required when speedo, gearbox is not fitted.
*Il faut, 4 quand un engrenage pour le compteur n'est pas monté.
*4 Sind Erforderlich Wenn Die Maschine Nicht Mit Tachogetrier Versehen Ist.
*Se requiere 4 cuando un engranaje para el velocimetro no es montado.

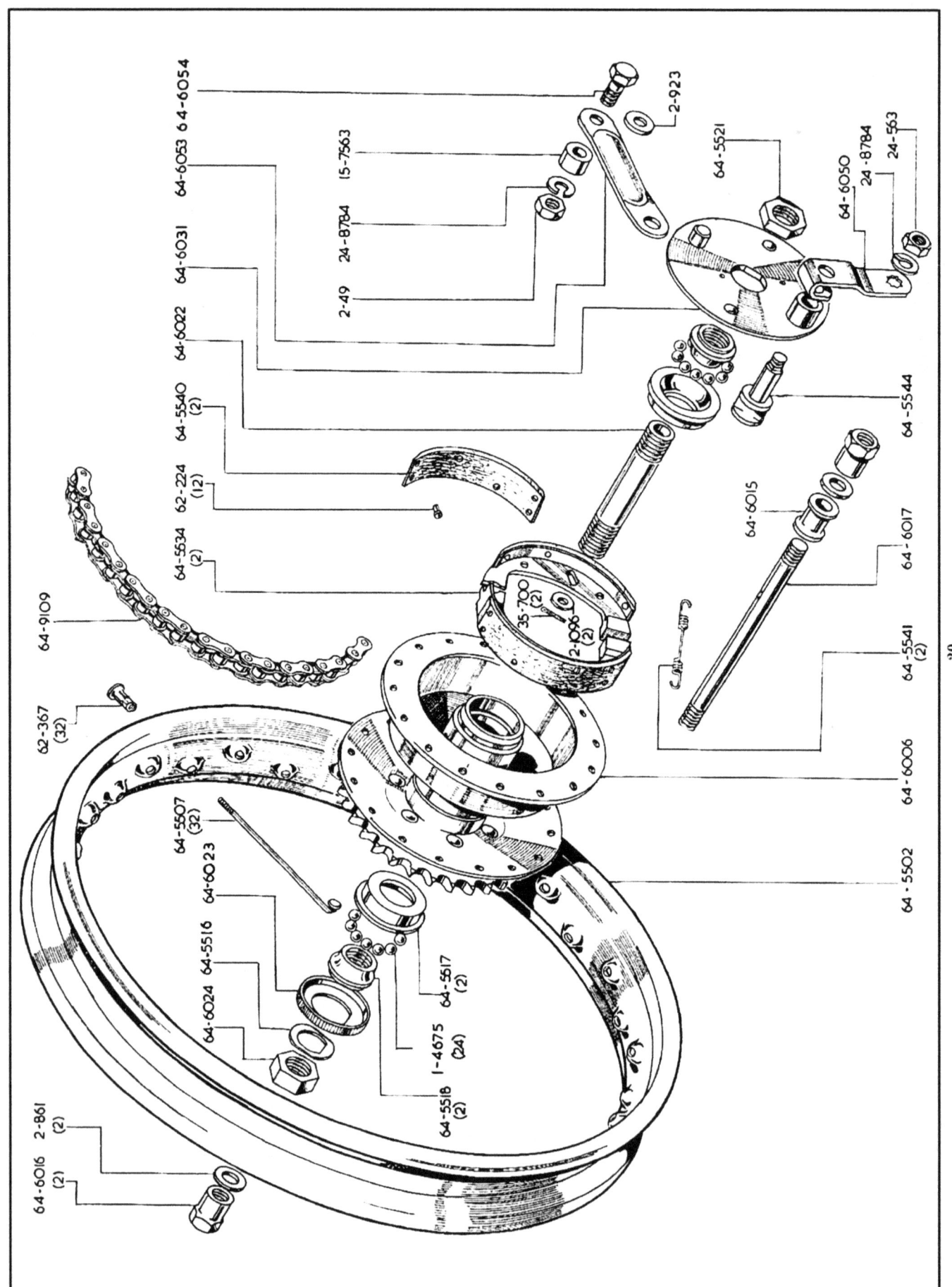

REAR WHEEL. ROUE AR. HINTERRAD. RUEDA TRASERA

Part No. Bestell-nr No. de parte	Description	Designation	Benennung	Descripción	Per Set Nombre Anzahl Juego de
1-4675	Ball	Bille	Kugel	Bola	24
2-49	Nut	Ecrou	Mutter	Tuerca	
2-861	Washer	Rondelle	Scheibe	Arandela	2
2-923	Washer	Rondelle	Scheibe	Arandela	
2-1096	Washer	Rondelle	Scheibe	Arandela	2
15-7563	Spacer Bush	Bague d'écartement	Distanzring	Anillo espaciador	
24-563	Nut	Ecrou	Mutter	Tuerca	2
24-8784	Lockwasher	Arrêtoir	Sicherung	Freno	2
35-700	Split Pin	Goupille	Splint	Chaveta hendida	2
62-224	Rivet	Rivet	Niet	Remache	12
62-367	Nipple	Ecrou	Nipple	Tuerca	32
64-5502	Rim	Jante	Felge	Llanta	
64-5507	Spoke	Rayon	Speiche	Raio	32
64-5516	Washer	Rondelle	Scheibe	Arandela	2
64-5517	Bearing Cup	Cuvette de roulement	Lagerschale	Copa de rolamiento	2
64-5518	Bearing Cone	Cone	Lagerkonus	Cona de cojinete	2
64-5521	Nut	Ecrou	Mutter	Tuerca	
64-5531	Brake Shoe	Segment	Bremsbacke	Zapata	2
64-5540	Brake Lining	Garniture	Belag	Guarnición	2
64-5541	Spring	Ressort	Feder	Resorte	2
64-5544	Brake Cam	Clé de frein	Bremsschlüssel	Llave de freno	
64-6001	Rear Wheel	Roue ar	Hinterrad	Rueda trasera	
64-6006	Rear Hub	Moyeu de roue ar	Hinterradnabe	Cubo de rueda tras	
64-6015	Spacer Bush	Bague d'écartement	Distanzring	Anillo espaciador	
64-6016	Nut	Ecrou	Mutter	Tuerca	2
64-6017	Axle	Axe	Achse	Eje	
64-6022	Spacer Tube	Tube entretoise	Abstandrohr	Tubo espaciador	
64-6023	Cap	Rondelle chapeau	Abdeckkappe	Tapon	
64-6024	Nut	Ecrou	Mutter	Tuerca	
64-6031	Brake Back Plate	Disque de frein	Bremsscheibe	Disco de freno	
64-6050	Brake Cam Lever	Levier de frein	Bremshebel	Palanca de freno	
64-6053	Anchor Strap	Ancrage de frein	Bremsanker	Anclaje de freno	
64-6054	Bolt	Boulon	Schraube	Tornillo	
64-9109	Chain	Chaîne	Kette	Cadena	

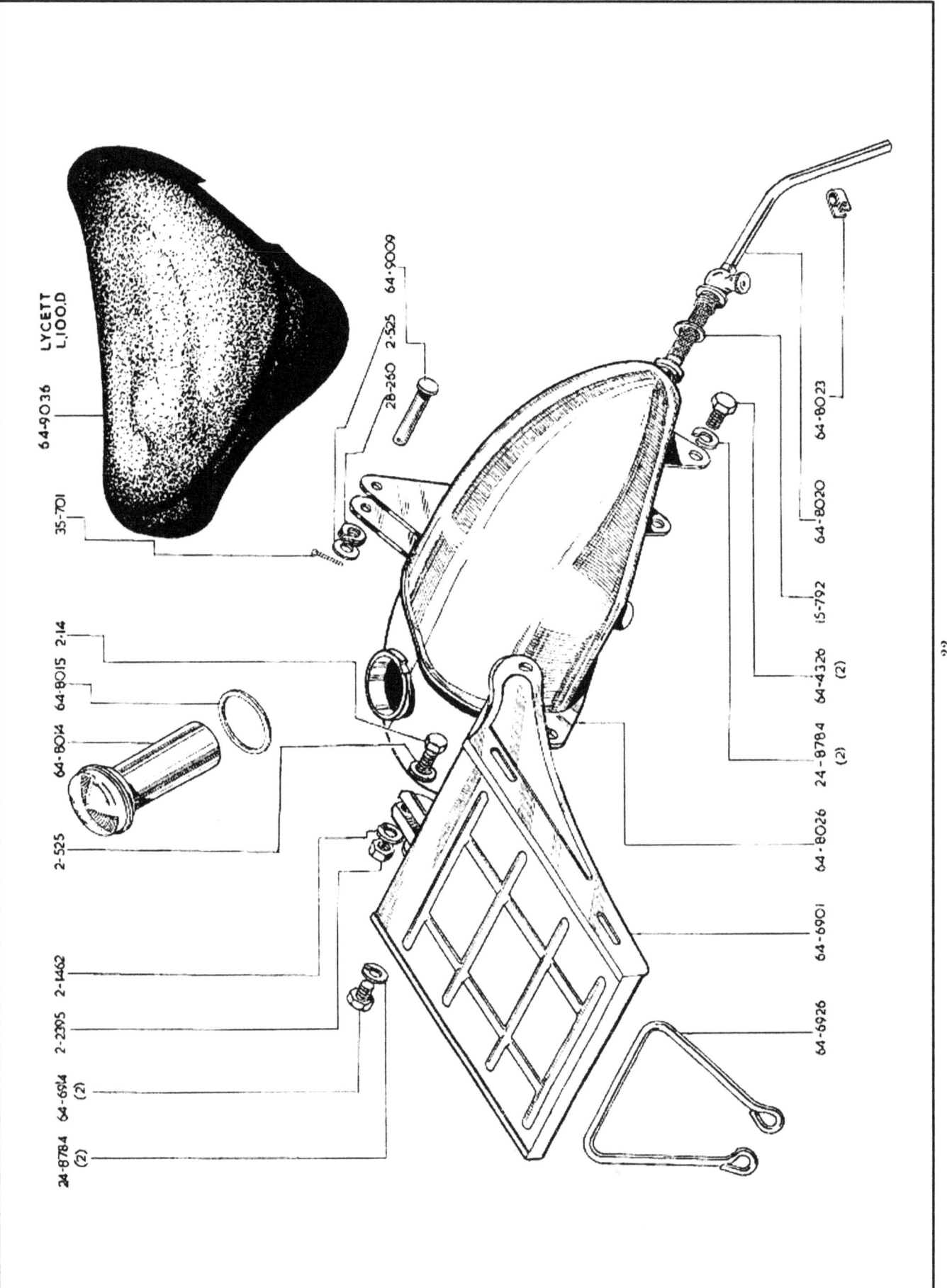

SADDLE, PETROL TANK, CARRIER. SELLE, RESERVOIR A CARBURANT, PORTE-BAGAGES
SATTEL, KRAFTSTOFFBEHALTER, GEPACKTRAGER
SILLIN, DEPOSITO de COMBUSTIBLE, PORTA EQUIPAJE

Part No. / No de commande / Bestell-nr / No. de parte	Description	Designation	Benennung	Descripción	Per Set / Nombre / Anzahl / Juego de
2-14	Bolt	Boulon	Schraube	Tornillo	
2-525	Washer	Rondelle	Scheibe	Arandela	2
2-1462	Lockwasher	Arrêtoir	Sicherung	Freno	
2-2395	Nut	Ecrou	Mutter	Tuerca	
15-792	Sealing Washer	Joint	Dichtung	Arandela de reten	4
24-8784	Lockwasher	Arrêtoir	Sicherung	Freno	
28-260	Spring Washer	Arrêtoir	Sicherung	Freno	
35-701	Split Pin	Goupille	Splint	Chaveta hendida	
64-4326	Bolt	Boulon	Schraube	Tornillo	
64-6901	Carrier	Porte-bagages	Gepäckträger	Porta equipaje	
64-6914	Bolt	Boulon	Schraube	Tornillo	2
64-6926	Lifting Handle	Poignée de levage	Hebegriff	Puño elevadoro	
64-8014	Filler Cap	Bouchon de réservoir	Verschluss	Tapa	
64-8015	Sealing Washer	Joint	Dichtung	Arandela de reten	
64-8020	Petrol Pipe and Tap	Tuyau à essence avec robinet	Benzinschlauch Mit Hahn	Caño de benzina con grifo	
64-8023	Clip Complete	Bride complète	Klammer Vollst	Grapa completa	
64-8026	Petrol Tank	Réservoir à carburant	Kraftstoffbehalter	Deposito de combustible	
64-9009	Pivot Pin	Axe	Bolzen	Eje	
64-9036	Saddle	Selle	Sattel	Sillin	

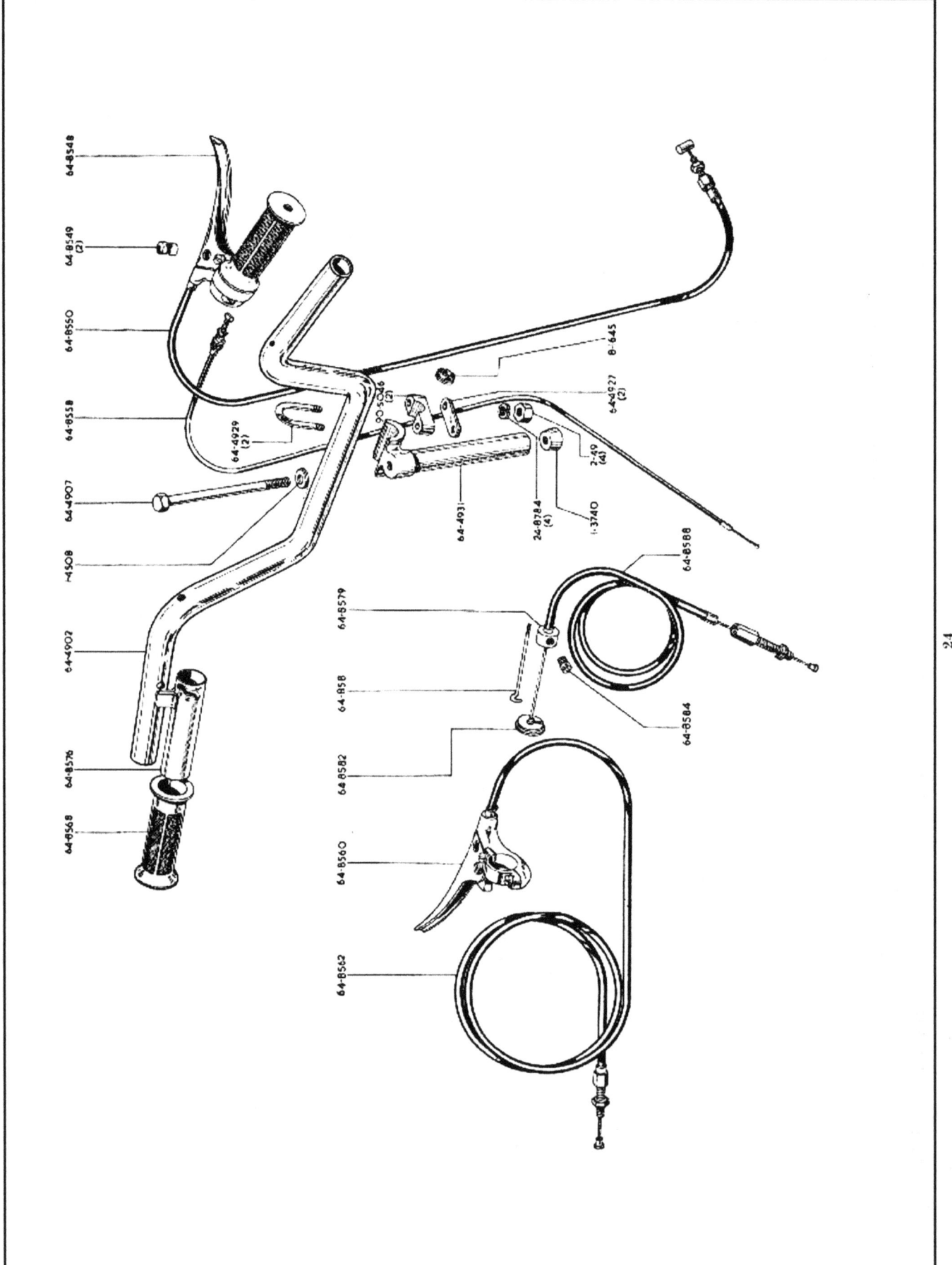

HANDLEBAR and CONTROLS. GUIDON ET COMMANDES
LENKER und STEURUNG. MANILLAR Y MANDOS

Part No. No de commande Bestell-nr No. de parte	Description	Designation	Benennung	Descripción	Per Set Nombre Anzahl Juego de
1-3740	Cone	Cone	Konus	Cono	
1-4508	Washer	Rondelle	Scheibe	Arandela	
2-4	Nut	Écrou	Mutter	Tuerca	4
8-1645	Rubber Grommet	Manchon caoutchouc	Gummitülle	Manguera de goma	4
24-8784	Lockwasher	Arrêtoir	Sicherun	Freno	
64-4902	Handlebar	Guidon	Lenker	Manillar	
64-4907	Bolt	Boulon	Schraube	Tornillo	2
64-4927	Plate	Plaque	Scheibe	Placa	2
64-4929	"U" Bolt	Boulon "U"	"U" Schraube	Tornillo "U"	
64-4931	Handlebar Stem	Tube du guidon	Lenkstange	Tubo del manillar	
61-8518	Brake Lever and Twist Grip	Levier de frein avec poignée tournante des gaz	Bremshebel Mit Vergaser-Drehgriff	Planca de freno y puño giratorio de gas	
64-8549	Cable Stop	Goupille d'arrêt	Sperrnippel	Boton retentor	2
64-8550	Front Brake Cable	Cable bowden de commande du frein avant.	Seilzug Fur Vorderradbremse	Cable bowden para freno delantero.	
64-8558	Throttle Cable	Cable bowden de commande du carburateur.	Seilzug Für Vergaser	Cable bowden para acelerador	
64-8560	Clutch Lever	Levier pour embrayage	Kupplungshebel	Palanca del embrague	
64-8562	Clutch Cable	Cable bowden de commande de l'embrayage.	Seilzug Für Kupplung	Cable bowden para embrague	
64-8568	Rubber Grip L/H	Poignée fixe de caoutchouc	Gummifest Griff	Puño fijo de goma	
64-8576	Gear Control Sleeve	Manchon du commande de vitesses	Hülse Für Getriebesel-Zug	Manguito del cable de comando de velocidades.	
64-8579	Cable Stop	Goupille d'arrêt	Sperrnippel	Boton retentor	
64-8581	Rod	Tringle	Zugstange	Varilla	
64-8582	End Cap	Capuchon de fermeture	Abschlusskappe	Tuza cerradora	
64-8584	Grub Screw	Cheville taravdée	Gewindestift	Tornillo prisionero	
61-8588	Gear Control Cable	Cable de commande des vitesse.	Seilzug Für Getriebe	Cable de comando de velocidades.	
90-5046	Clamp	Bride	Lasche	Brida	2

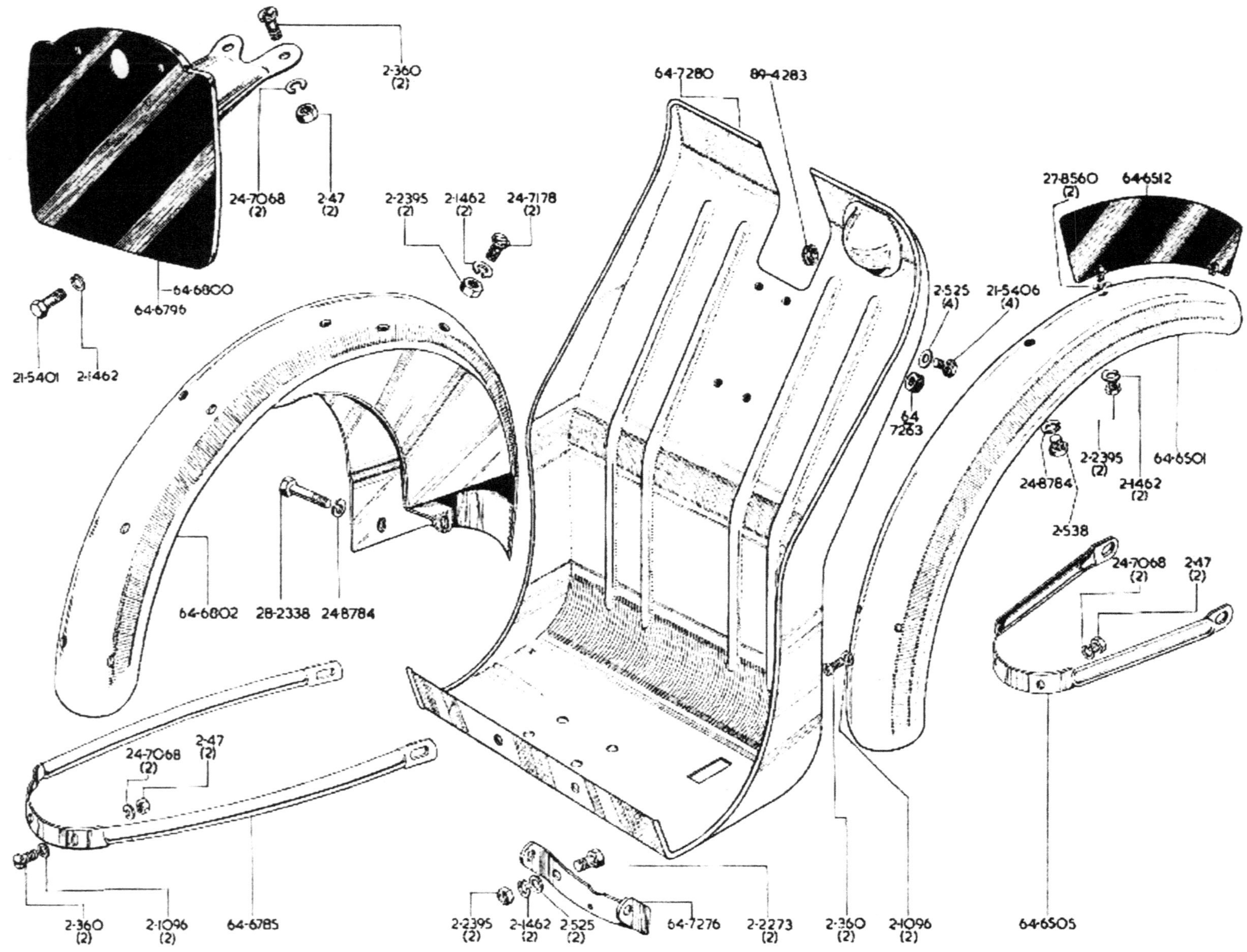
2·360 (2)
64·7280
89·4283
24·7068 (2)
2·47 (2)
2·2395 (2)
2·1462 (2)
24·7178 (2)
27·8560 (2)
64·6512
64·6800
64·6796
2·525 (4)
21·5406 (4)
21·5401
2·1462
64·7263
2·2395 (2)
64·6501
24·8784
2·1462 (2)
2·538
24·7068 (2)
2·47 (2)
64·6802
28·2338
24·8784
24·7068 (2)
2·47 (2)
2·360 (2)
2·1096 (2)
64·6785
2·2395 (2)
2·1462 (2)
2·525 (2)
64·7276
2·2273 (2)
2·360 (2)
2·1096 (2)
64·6505

LEGSHIELDS, MUDGUARDS. PROTEGE-JAMBES et GARDEBOUE.
BEINSCHILD und SCHUTZBLECHE. GUARDAPIERNAS Y GUARDABARROS

Part No. / No de commande / Bestell-nr / No. de parte	Description	Designation	Benennung	Descripción	Per Set / Nombre / Anzahl / Juego de
2 47	Nut	Ecrou	Mutter	Tuerca	6
2 360	Screw	Vis	Schraube	Tornillo	6
2 525	Washer	Rondelle	Scheibe	Arandela	6
2 538	Bolt	Boulon	Schraube	Tornillo	
2 1096	Washer	Rondelle	Scheibe	Arandela	4
2 1462	Lockwasher	Arrêtoir	Sicherung	Freno	7
2 2273	Bolt	Boulon	Schraube	Tornillo	2
2 2395	Nut	Ecrou	Mutter	Tuerca	6
21 5401	Bolt	Boulon	Schraube	Tornillo	
21 5406	Bolt	Boulon	Schraube	Tornillo	4
24-7068	Lockwasher	Arrêtoir	Sicherung	Freno	6
24-7178	Screw	Vis	Schraube	Tornillo	2
24-8784	Lockwasher	Arrêtoir	Sicherung	Freno	2
27-8560	Washer	Rondelle	Scheibe	Arandela	2
28-2338	Bolt	Boulon	Schraube	Tornillo	2
64-6501	Front Mudguard	Guard-boue de roue av	Vorderradschutzblech	Guardabarro del	
64-6505	Front Stay	Tringle av	Vorderstrebe	Tirante del	
64-6512	No. Plate	Plaque de police	Kennzeichenschild	Chapa de patente	
64-6785	Rear Stay	Tringle ar	Hinterstrebe	Tirante tras	
64-6796	No. Plate (Lucas)	Plaque de police (Lucas)	Kennzeichenschild (Lucas)	Chapa de patente (Lucas)	
64-6800	No. Plate (Wipac)	Plaque de police (Wipac)	Kennzeichenschild (Wipac)	Chapa de patente (Wipac)	
64-6802	Rear Guard	Guard-boue de roue ar	Hinterradschutzblech	Guardabarro tras	
64-7263	Spacer Bush	Bague d'écartement	Distanzring	Anillo espaciador	
64-7276	Bracket	Support	Lagerbock	Soporte	
64-7280	Legshield	Protege-jambe	Beinschild	Guardapiernas	
89-4283	Rubber Grommet	Manchon caoutchouc	Gummihülle	Manguera de goma	

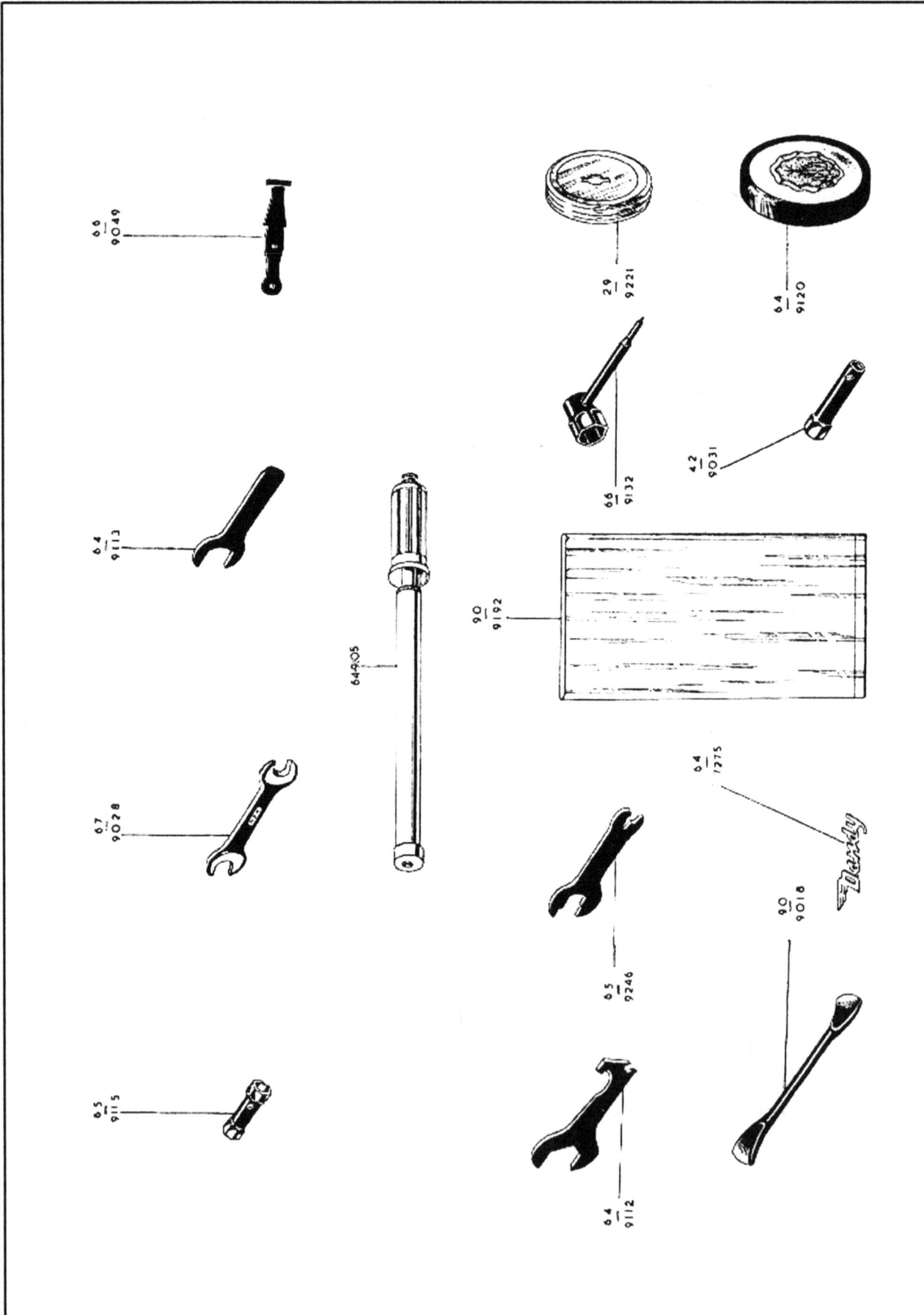

TOOLS. OUTILS. WERKZEUGER. HERRAMIENTOS

Part No. / No. de commande / Bestell-nr / No. de parte	Description	Designation	Benennung	Descripción	Per Set / Nombre / Anzahl / Juego de
29-9221	Licence Holder	Porte permet	Licenzhalter	Portalicencia	
42-9031	Box Spanner	Clé à douille	Steckschlüssel	Llave de tubo	
64-7275	Name Plate	Ecusson "Dandy"	Typzeichen "Dandy"	Placa "Dandy"	
64-9105	Inflator	Pompe à air	Luftpumpe	Bomba de aire	
64-9112	Double Ended Spanner	Clé à fourche double	Doppelschraubenschlüssel	Llave de dos bocas	
64-9113	Spanner	Clé à écrous	Schraubenschlüssel	Llave de tuercas	
64-9115	Tool Kit Complete	Outillage complete	Werkzeug Vollst	Herramientos comp.	
64-9120	Badge	Ecusson	Firmenzeichen	Emblema	
65-9115	Box Spanner	Clé à douille	Steckschlüssel	Llave de tubo	
66-9246	Double Ended Spanner	Clé à fourche double	Doppelschraubenschlüssel	Llave de dos bocas	
66-9049	Rubber Band	Bande caoutchouc	Gummiband	Cinta de goma	
67-9132	Box Spanner	Clé à douille	Steckschlüssel	Llave de tubo	
67-9028	Double Ended Spanner	Clé à fourche double	Doppelschraubenschlüssel	Llave de dos bocas	
90-9018	Tyre Lever	Démonte-pneu	Reifenheber	Palanca Desmonta-neumaticos.	
90-9192	Tool Bag	Trousse à outils	Werkzeughülle	Bolsa de herramientos	

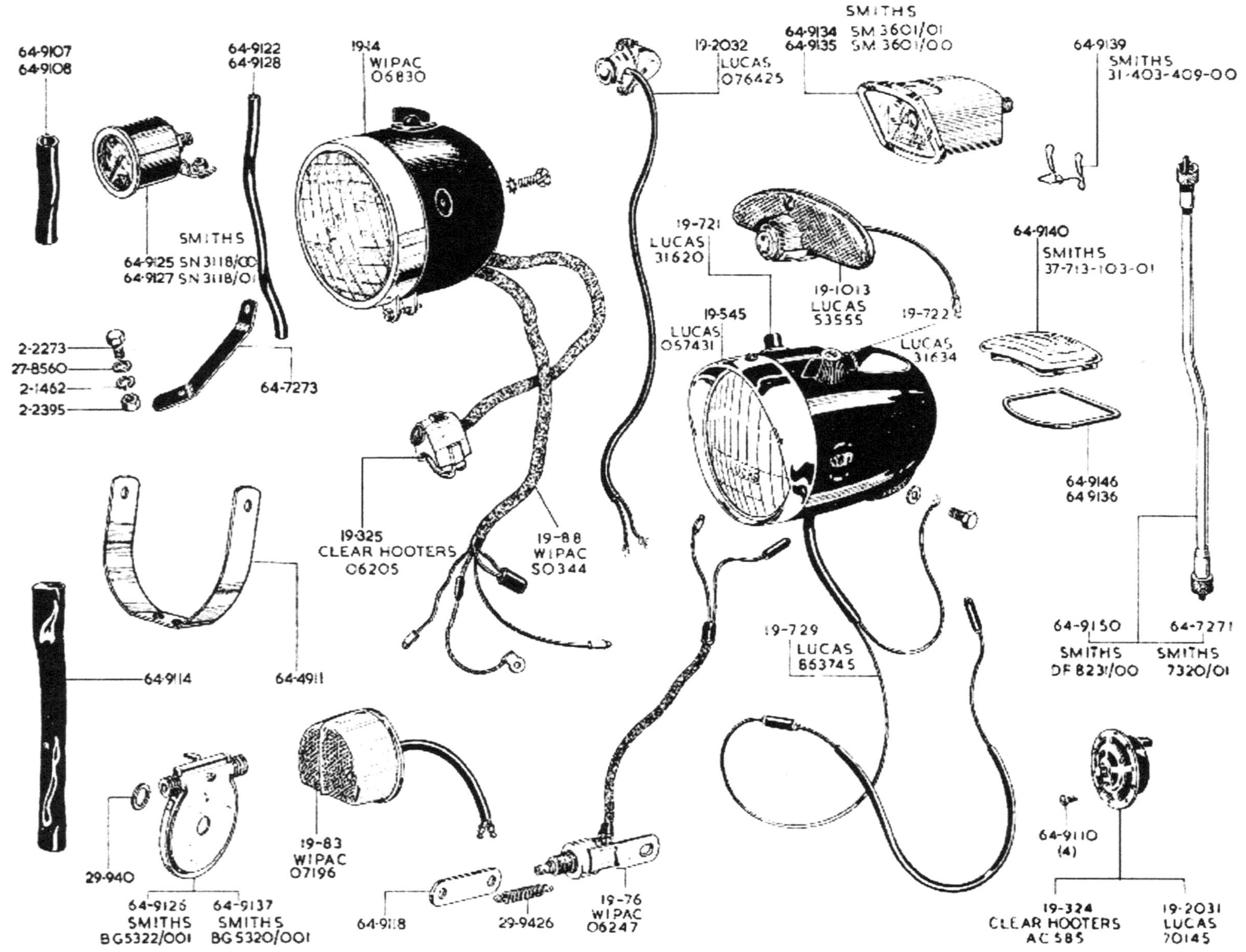
64-9107
64-9108
64-9122
64-9128
19-14
WIPAC
06830
19-2032
LUCAS
076425
SMITHS
64-9134 SM 3601/01
64-9135 SM 3601/00
64-9139
SMITHS
31-403-409-00
SMITHS
64-9125 SN 3118/00
64-9127 SN 3118/01
19-721
LUCAS
31620
19-1013
LUCAS
53555
64-9140
SMITHS
37-713-103-01
2-2273
27-8560
2-1462
2-2395
64-7273
19-545
LUCAS
057431
19-722
LUCAS
31634
64-9146
64 9136
19-325
CLEAR HOOTERS
06205
19-88
WIPAC
SO344
64-9150
SMITHS
DF 8231/00
64-7271
SMITHS
7320/01
19-729
LUCAS
863745
64-9114
64-4911
29-940
64-9126
SMITHS
BG5322/001
64-9137
SMITHS
BG 5320/001
19-83
WIPAC
07196
64-9118
29-9426
19-76
WIPAC
06247
64-9110
(4)
19-324
CLEAR HOOTERS
AC 585
19-2031
LUCAS
70145

ELECTRICAL and SUNDRIES. EQUIPEMENT ELECTRIQUE et PIECE VARIEES
ELEKTR. AUSRUSTUNG und SONSTIGE TEILE. EQUIP ELECTRICO Y PIEZAS VARIAS

Part No. No de commande Bestell-nr No. de parte	Description	Designation	Benennung	Descripción	Per Set Nombre Anzahl Juego de
2-1462	Lockwasher	Arrêtoir	Sicherung	Freno	
2-2273	Bolt	Boulon	Schraube	Tornillo	
2-2395	Nut	Ecrou	Mutter	Tuerca	
19-14	Headlamp Complete (Wipac)	Phare complète (Wipac)	Scheinwerfer Komp. (Wipac)	Faro completa (Wipac)	
19-76	Stop Lamp Switch	Interrupteur de feu "Stop"	Bremslichtschalter	Interruptor para la luz "Stop"	
19-83	Rear Lamp (Wipac)	Feu rouge arrière (Wipac)	Schlusslampe (Wipac)	Luz roja trasera (Wipac)	
19-324	Horn (Wipac)	Avertisseur (Wipac)	Signalhorn (Wipac)	Bocina (Wipac)	
19-325	Horn and Dipper Switch	Commutateur code avec bouton d'avertisseur	Abblendschalter Mit Horndruckknopf.	Conmutador de cruce con pulsador de bocina.	
19-515	Headlamp Complete (Lucas)	Phare complète (Lucas)	Scheinwerfer Komp. (Lucas)	Faro completa (Lucas)	1
19-721	Dipper Switch (Lucas)	Commutateur de code (Lucas)	Abblendschalter (Lucas)	Conmutador de cruce (Lucas)	
19-1013	Rear Lamp (Lucas)	Feu rouge arrière (Lucas)	Schlusslampe (Lucas)	Luz roja trasera (Lucas)	
19-2031	Horn (Lucas)	Avertisseur (Lucas)	Signalhorn (Lucas)	Bocina (Lucas)	
19-2032	Horn Push (Lucas)	Bouton d'avertisseur (Lucas)	Hornknopf (Lucas)	Botón de bocina (Lucas)	
27-8560	Washer	Rondelle	Scheibe	Arandela	
29-910	Washer	Rondelle	Scheibe	Arandela	
29-9426	Spring	Ressort	Feder	Resorte	
64-4911	Bracket	Support	Lagerbock	Soporte	
64-7271	Speedo Cable (for 64-9130/1)	Flexible d'entraînement (pour 64-9130/1)	Antriebswelle (für 64-9130/1)	Arbol de transmisión (para 64-9130/1)	4
64-7273	Bracket	Support	Lagerbock	Soporte	
64-9107	Plastic Sleeve (lower)	Manchon plastique inférieur	Kunststoffhülse (Unten)	Manguito plástico (inf)	
64-9108	Plastic Sleeve (upper)	Manchon plastique supérieur	Kunststoffhülse (Oben)	Manguito plástico (sup)	
64-9110	Screw	Vis	Schraube	Tornillo	
64-9114	Plastic Sleeve	Manchon plastique	Kunststoffhülse	Manguito plástico	
64-9118	Plate	Plaque	Scheibe	Placa	
64-9122	Plastic Sleeve (short)	Manchon plastique (court)	Kunststoffhülse (Kurz)	Manguito plástico (corto)	
64-9125	Speedo Head (for 64-9130)	Compteur de vitesse (pour 64-9130)	Tachometer (Für 64-9130)	Velocímetro (para 64-9130)	
64-9126	Speedo G/Box (for 64-9130.1)	Entraînement du compteur (pour 64-9130.1)	Tachoantrieb (Für 64-9130.1)	Accionamiento del velocímetro (para 64-9130/1)	
64-9127	Speedo Head (for 64-9131)	Compteur de vitesse (pour 64-9131)	Tachometer (Für 64-9131)	Velocímetro (para 64-9131)	
64-9128	Plastic Sleeve (long)	Manchon plastique (long)	Kunststoffhülse (Lang)	Manguito plástico (largo)	
64-9130	Speedo Complete (m.p.h.)	Compteur de vitesse complète (m.p.h.)	Tachometer Komp. (m.p.h.)	Velocímetro comp. (m.p.h.)	
64-9131	Speedo Complete (k.p.h.)	Compteur de vitesse complète (k.p.h.)	Tachometer Komp. (k.p.h.)	Velocímetro comp. (k.p.h.)	
64-9132	Speedo Complete (m.p.h.)	Compteur de vitesse complète (m.p.h.)	Tachometer Komp. (m.p.h.)	Velocímetro comp. (m.p.h.)	
64-9133	Speedo Complete (k.p.h.)	Compteur de vitesse complète (k.p.h.)	Tachometer Komp. (k.p.h.)	Velocímetro comp. (k.p.h.)	
64-9134	Speedo Head (for 64-9133)	Compteur de vitesse (pour 64-9133)	Tachometer (Für 64-9133)	Velocímetro (para 64-9133)	
64-9135	Speedo Head (for 64-9132)	Compteur de vitesse (pour 64-9132)	Tachometer (Für 64-9132)	Velocímetro (para 64-9132)	
64-9136	Rubber Moulding (for 64-9132/3)	Profilé caoutchouc (pour 64-9132/3)	Profilgummi (Für 64-9132/3)	Perfil de goma (para 64-9132/3)	
64-9137	Speedo G/Box (for 64-9132/3)	Entraînement du compteur (pour 64-9132/3)	Tachoantrieb (Für 64-9132/3)	Accionamiento del velocímetro (para 64-9132/3)	
64-9139	Wire Clip (for 64-9140)	Agrafe	Spannbügel	Estribo	
64-9140	Plastic Cover	Couvercle plastique	Kunststoffdeckel	Tapa plástica	
64-9146	Rubber Moulding (for 64-9140)	Profile caoutchouc (pour 64-9140)	Profilgummi (Für 64-9140)	Perfil de goma (para 64-9140)	
64-9150	Speedo Cable (for 64-9132/3)	Flexible d'entraînement (pour 64-9132/3)	Antriebswelle (für 64-9132/3)	Arbol de transmisión (para 64-9132/3)	

*For Legshield fitting.
†For Headlamp fitting.

*Pour montage sur protège-jambe.
†Pour montage sur phare.

*Zur Anbringung An Beinschutz
†Zur Anbringung An den scheinwerfer.

*Para montaje en el guardapiernas.
†Para montaje en el faro.

PISTONS
PISTONS
KOLBEN
EMBOLOS

PISTON COMPLETE PISTON COMPLETE KOLBEN VOLLST EMBOLO COMP		
Standard Standard Standard Standard	+ .015" + .381 mm.	+ .030" + .769 mm.
64-40	64-43	64-45

PISTON RING SEGMENT VERDICHTUNGSRING SEGMENTO		
Standard Standard Standard	+ .015" + .381 mm.	+ .030" + .769 mm.
64-50 (2)	64-51 (2)	64-52 (2)

CARBURETTER SETTINGS
REGLAGE DU CARBURATEUR
EINSTELLUNG DES VERGASERS
AJUSTE REL CARBURADOR

B.S.A. Part No. No. de pièce B.S.A. B.S.A. Bestell-Nr No. de pieza B.S.A.	Makers Part No. No. du fabricant Nr-Hersteller No.-fabricante	Choke Size Admission d'air Luft Einlass Entrada de aire	Main Jet Gicleur principal Hauptdüse Gicleur principal	Throttle Slide Rousseau des gaz Drossel Schieber Correcizo de aceleración	Needle Position Pos. aiguille Nadelem-Stellung Pos. aguja	Needle Jet Gicleur à aiguille Nadeldüse Gicleur de aguja
19-2337	365/1	½" (12.7 mm.)	35 c.c	3	3	.0745" (1.91 mm.)

ELECTRICAL EQUIPMENT
EQUIPEMENT ELECTRIQUE
ELEKTRISCHE AUSRUSTUNG
EQUIPO ELECTRICO

JOSEPH LUCAS LTD., GREAT KING STREET, BIRMINGHAM, ENGLAND.

THE WIPAC GROUP, BLETCHLEY, ENGLAND.

CLEAR HOOTERS LTD., 33, HAMPTON STREET, BIRMINGHAM 19, ENGLAND.

SPARK PLUGS
BOUGIES
ZUNDKERZEN
BUJIAS

CHAMPION SPARKING PLUG CO. LTD., FELTHAM, MIDDLESEX, ENGLAND.

SPEEDOMETERS
COMPTEURS DE VITESSES
TACHOMETER
VELOCIMETROS

SMITH'S MOTOR ACCESSORIES, CRICKLEWOOD WORKS, LONDON, ENGLAND.

CARBURETTERS
CARBURATEURS
VERGASER
CARBURADORES

AMAL LTD., HOLFORD ROAD, WITTON, BIRMINGHAM 6, ENGLAND.

VELOCEPRESS MANUALS – MOTORCYCLE BY MAKE

AJS 1932-1948 SINGLES & TWINS 250cc THRU 1000cc (BOOK OF)
AJS 1945-1960 SINGLES 350cc & 500cc MODELS 16 & 18 (BOOK OF)
AJS 1955-1965 SINGLES 350cc & 500cc (BOOK OF)
AJS 1957-1966 FACTORY WSM - ALL SINGLES & TWINS
ARIEL UP TO 1932 (BOOK OF)
ARIEL 1932-1939 PREWAR MODELS (BOOK OF)
ARIEL 1933-1951 (WORKSHOP MANUAL)
ARIEL 1939-1960 4 STROKE SINGLES (BOOK OF)
ARIEL 1958-1964 LEADER & ARROW (BOOK OF)
BMW R26 R27 (1956-1967) FACTORY WORKSHOP MANUAL
BMW R50 R50S R60 R69S (1955-1969) FACTORY WORKSHOP MANUAL
BRIDGESTONE 90 SERIES FACTORY WSM & PARTS CATALOGUE
BRIDGESTONE 175 SERIES FACTORY WSM & PARTS CATALOGUE
BRIDGESTONE 350 SERIES FACTORY WSM & PARTS CATALOGUES
BSA SERVICE SHEETS MASTER CATALOGUE ALL MODELS 1945-1967
BSA BANTAM D1 TO D7 1948-1966 FACTORY SERVICE SHEETS MANUAL
BSA BANTAM ALL MODELS FROM 1948 ONWARDS (BOOK OF)
BSA BANTAM D14 FACTORY WORKSHOP & INSTRUCTION MANUAL
BSA DANDY FACTORY WORKSHOP MANUAL COMPILATION
BSA SINGLES & V-TWINS UP TO 1927 (BOOK OF)
BSA SINGLES & V-TWINS UP TO 1930 (BOOK OF)
BSA SINGLES & V-TWINS UP TO 1935 (BOOK OF)
BSA SINGLES & V-TWINS 1936-1939 (BOOK OF)
BSA C10, C11 & C12 1945-1958 FACTORY SERVICE SHEETS MANUAL
BSA OHV & SV SINGLES 250-600cc 1945-1959 (BOOK OF)
BSA C15 & B40 1958-1967 FACTORY SERVICE SHEETS MANUAL
BSA OHV & SV SINGLES 250cc (ONLY) 1954-1970 (BOOK OF)
BSA B31, B32, B33 & B34 1945-60 FACTORY SERVICE SHEETS MANUAL
BSA OHV SINGLES 350 & 500cc 1955-1967 (BOOK OF)
BSA M20, M21 & M33 1945-1963 FACTORY SERVICE SHEETS MANUAL
BSA TWINS A7 & A10 1948-1962 FACTORY SERVICE SHEETS MANUAL
BSA TWINS A7 & A10 1948-1962 (BOOK OF)
BSA TWINS A50 & A65 1962-1965 FACTORY WORKSHOP MANUAL
BSA TWINS A50 & A65 1962-1969 (SECOND BOOK OF)
DOUGLAS 1929-1939 PREWAR ALL MODELS (BOOK OF)
DOUGLAS 1948-1957 POSTWAR ALL MODELS FACTORY SHOP MANUAL
DUCATI 160cc, 250cc & 350cc OHC MODELS FACTORY SHOP MANUAL
HONDA 50 ALL MODELS UP TO 1970 INC MONKEY & TRAIL (BOOK OF)
HONDA 90 ALL MODELS UP TO 1966 (BOOK OF)
HONDA 125-150cc TWINS C/CS/CB/CA FACTORY WORKSHOP MANUAL
HONDA 250-305 TWINS C/CS/CB 1959-1967 FACTORY WSM
HOHDA 250-350 TWINS CB/CL/SL 1968-1973 FACTORY WSM
HONDA 450 CB/CL 1965-1974 K0 TO K7 FACTORY WORKSHOP MANUAL
HONDA C100 SUPER CUB FACTORY WORKSHOP MANUAL
HONDA C110 SPORT CUB 1962-1969 FACTORY WORKSHOP MANUAL
HONDA TWINS & SINGLES 50cc THRU 305cc 1960-1966 (BOOK OF)
HONDA TWINS ALL MODELS 125cc THRU 450cc UP TO 1968 (BOOK OF)
INDIAN PONYBIKE, BOY RACER & PAPOOSE ILL PARTS LIST & SALES LIT
J.A.P. ENGINES 1927-1952 & MOTORCYCLES 1934-1952 (BOOK OF)
MATCHLESS 1931-1939 ALL MODELS 250cc THRU 990cc (BOOK OF)
MATCHLESS 1945-1956 350 & 500cc SINGLES (BOOK OF)
MATCHLESS 1955-1966 350 & 500cc SINGLES (BOOK OF)
MATCHLESS 1957-1966 FACTORY WSM - ALL SINGLES & TWINS
NEW IMPERIAL ALL SV & OHV FROM 1935 ONWARDS (BOOK OF)
NORTON 1932-1939 PREWAR MODELS (BOOK OF)
NORTON 1932-1947 (BOOK OF)
NORTON 1938-1956 (BOOK OF)
NORTON 1955-1963 MODELS 19, 50 & ES2 (BOOK OF)
NORTON 1955-1965 DOMINATOR TWINS (BOOK OF)
NORTON 1960-1970 TWIN CYLINDER FACTORY WORKSHOP MANUAL
NORTON 1970-1975 COMMANDO FACTORY WORKSHOP MANUAL
NORTON 1975-1978 MK 3 COMMANDO FACTORY WORKSHOP MANUAL
PANTHER 1932-1958 LIGHTWEIGHT MODELS 250 & 350cc (BOOK OF)
PANTHER 1938-1966 HEAVYWEIGHT MODELS 600 & 650cc (BOOK OF)
RALEIGH MOTORCYCLES 1919-1933 (BOOK OF)
ROYAL ENFIELD 1934-1946 SINGLES & V TWINS (BOOK OF)
ROYAL ENFIELD 1937-1953 SINGLES & V TWINS (BOOK OF)
ROYAL ENFIELD 1946-1962 SINGLES (BOOK OF)
ROYAL ENFIELD 1958-1966 250cc & 350cc SINGLES (SECOND BOOK OF)
ROYAL ENFIELD 736cc INTERCEPTOR FACTORY WORKSHOP MANUAL
RUDGE 1933-1939 (BOOK OF)
SUNBEAM 1928-1939 (BOOK OF)
SUNBEAM 1946-1957 S7 & S8 (BOOK OF)
SUZUKI 50cc & 80cc UP TO 1966 (BOOK OF)
SUZUKI T10 1963-1967 FACTORY WORKSHOP MANUAL
SUZUKI T20 & T200 1965-1969 FACTORY WORKSHOP MANUAL
SUZUKI TWINS 1962 ONWARDS 125-500cc WORKSHOP MANUAL
TRIUMPH 1935-1939 PREWAR MODELS (BOOK OF)
TRIUMPH 1935-1949 (BOOK OF)
TRIUMPH 1937-1951 (WORKSHOP MANUAL)
TRIUMPH 1945-1955 FACTORY WORKSHOP MANUAL
TRIUMPH 1945-1958 TWINS (BOOK OF)
TRIUMPH 1956-1969 TWINS (BOOK OF)
VELOCETTE 1925-1970 ALL SINGLES & TWINS (BOOK OF)
VILLIERS ENGINE UP TO 1959 INC. 3 WHEELERS (BOOK OF)
VILLIERS ENGINE UP TO 1969 (BOOK OF)
VINCENT 1935-1955 (WORKSHOP MANUAL)
YAMAHA 1961-1967 YA5 & YA6 (WORKSHOP MANUAL & ILL PARTS LIST)
YAMAHA 1971-1972 JT1& JT2 (WORKSHOP MANUAL & ILL PARTS LIST)

VELOCEPRESS TECHNICAL BOOKS – MOTORCYCLE

1930'S BRITISH MOTORCYCLE CARBS & ELEC COMPONENTS (BOOK OF)
1930'S BRITISH MOTORCYCLE ENGINES (OVERHAUL & MAINTENANCE)
1930'S BRITISH MOTORCYCLE GEARBOXES & CLUTCHES (BOOK OF)
CATALOG OF BRITISH MOTORCYCLES (1951 MODELS)
LUCAS ELECTRONICS BRITISH M/CYCLES REPAIR & PARTS (1950-1977)
MOTORCYCLE ENGINEERING (P.E. Irving)
MOTORCYCLE ROAD TESTS 1949-1953 (Motor Cycle Magazine UK)
SPEED AND HOW TO OBTAIN IT (Motor Cycle Magazine UK)
TUNING FOR SPEED (P.E. Irving)
WIPAC SERVICE MANUAL NUMBER 3

VELOCEPRESS MANUALS – SCOOTERS BY MAKE

BSA SUNBEAM SCOOTER WORKSHOP MANUAL 1959-1965
BSA SUNBEAM SCOOTER 1959-1965 (BOOK OF)
LAMBRETTA 1947-1957 ALL 125 & 150cc MODELS (BOOK OF)
LAMBRETTA 1957-1970 LI & TV MODELS (SECOND BOOK OF)
NSU PRIMA 1956-1964 ALL MODELS (BOOK OF)
TRIUMPH TIGRESS SCOOTER WORKSHOP MANUAL 1959-1965
TRIUMPH TIGRESS SCOOTER (BOOK OF)
VESPA 1951-1961 (BOOK OF)
VESPA 1955-1963 125 & 150cc & GS MODELS (SECOND BOOK OF)
VESPA 1955-1968 GS & SS (BOOK OF)
VESPA 1963-1972 90, 125 & 150cc (THIRD BOOK OF)

VELOCEPRESS MANUALS – MOPEDS & MOTORIZED BICYCLES

CYCLEMOTOR (BOOK OF)
NSU QUICKLY 1953-1963 ALL MODELS (BOOK OF)
PUCH MAXI N & S MAINTENANCE & REPAIR (3 MANUAL COMPILATION)
RALEIGH MOPEDS 1960-1969 (BOOK OF)

VELOCEPRESS MANUALS - THREE WHEELER'S

BOND MINICAR THREE WHEELER 1948-1967 (BOOK OF)
BMW ISETTA FACTORY WORKSHOP MANUAL
BSA THREE WHEELER (BOOK OF)
RELIANT REGAL THREE WHEELER 1952-1973 (BOOK OF)
VINTAGE MORGAN THREE WHEELER (BOOK OF)

VELOCEPRESS MANUALS – AUTOMOBILE BY MAKE

ALFA ROMEO GIULIA WORKSHOP MANUAL 1300 TO 2000cc 1962-1975
ALFA ROMEO GIULIA TECH MANUAL CARBURETED CARS FROM 1962
ALFA ROMEO GIULIA TECH MANUAL FUEL INJECTED CARS FROM 1969
ALFA ROMEO GIULIETTA & GIULIA 750 & 101 SERIES 1955-1965 WSM
AUSTIN-HEALEY SPRITE & MG MIDGET WORKSHOP MANUAL 1958-1971
BMW 600 LIMOUSINE FACTORY WORKSHOP MANUAL
BMW 600 LIMOUSINE OWNERS HAND BOOK & SERVICE MANUAL
BMW 2000 & 2002 1966-1976 WORKSHOP MANUAL
CORVAIR 1960-1969 WORKSHOP MANUAL
CORVETTE V8 1955-1962 WORKSHOP MANUAL
FIAT 500 FACTORY WORKSHOP MANUAL 1957-1973
FIAT 600, 600D & MULTIPLA FACTORY WORKSHOP MANUAL 1955-1969
JAGUAR E-TYPE 3.8 & 4.2 SERIES 1 & 2 WORKSHOP MANUAL
JAGUAR MK 7, 8, 9 & XK120, 140, 150 WORKSHOP MANUAL 1948-1961
METROPOLITAN FACTORY WORKSHOP MANUAL
MGA & MGB OWNERS HANDBOOK & WORKSHOP MANUAL
MG MIDGET TC, TD, TF & TF1500 WORKSHOP MANUAL
PORSCHE 356 1948-1965 WORKSHOP MANUAL
PORSCHE 911 2.0, 2.2, 2.4 LITRE 1964-1973 WORKSHOP MANUAL
PORSCHE 911 2.7, 3.0, 3.2 LITRE 1973-1989 WORKSHOP MANUAL
PORSCHE 912 WORKSHOP MANUAL
TRIUMPH TR2, TR3, TR4 1953-1965 WORKSHOP MANUAL
VOLKSWAGEN TRANSPORTER, TRUCKS & WAGONS 1950-1979 WSM
VOLVO 1944-1968 ALL MODELS WORKSHOP MANUAL

VELOCEPRESS TECHNICAL BOOKS - AUTOMOBILE

FERRARI 250/GT SERVICE AND MAINTENANCE
FERRARI GUIDE TO PERFORMANCE
FERRARI OWNER'S HANDBOOK
FERRARI TUNING TIPS & MAINTENANCE TECHNIQUES
HOW TO BUILD A FIBERGLASS CAR
HOW TO BUILD A RACING CAR
HOW TO RESTORE THE MODEL 'A' FORD
MASERATI OWNER'S HANDBOOK
OBERT'S FIAT GUIDE
PERFORMANCE TUNING THE SUNBEAM TIGER
SOUPING THE VOLKSWAGEN
SOLEX CARBURETORS (EMPHASIS ON UK & EU AUTOMOBILES)
SU CARBURETORS (EMPHASIS ON UK AUTOMOBILES)
WEBER CARBURETORS (EMPHASIS ON ALFA & FIAT)

VELOCEPRESS BOOKS & GUIDES - AUTOMOBILE

ABARTH BUYERS GUIDE
COMPLETE CATALOG OF JAPANESE MOTOR VEHICLES
FERRARI 308 SERIES BUYER'S AND OWNER'S GUIDE
FERRARI BERLINETTA LUSSO
FERRARI BROCHURES AND SALES LITERATURE 1946-1967
FERRARI BROCHURES AND SALES LITERATURE 1968-1989
FERRARI SERIAL NUMBERS PART I - ODD NUMBERS TO 21399
FERRARI SERIAL NUMBERS PART II - EVEN NUMBERS TO 1050
FERRARI SPYDER CALIFORNIA
HENRY'S FABULOUS MODEL "A" FORD
MASERATI BROCHURES AND SALES LITERATURE

VELOCEPRESS BOOKS – RACING

CARRERA PANAMERICANA - MEXICAN ROAD RACE (BOOK OF)
DIALED IN - THE JAN OPPERMAN STORY
IF HEMINGWAY HAD WRITTEN A RACING NOVEL
VEDA ORR'S NEW REVISED HOT ROD PICTORIAL

AUTOBOOKS WORKSHOP MANUALS & BROOKLANDS ROAD TEST PORTFOLIOS

FOR A COMPLETE LISTING OF THE AUTOBOOKS & BROOKLANDS TITLES THAT WE CURRENTLY HAVE AVAILABLE, PLEASE VISIT OUR WEBSITE.

www.VelocePress.com

www.ingramcontent.com/pod-product-compliance
Lightning Source LLC
Chambersburg PA
CBHW080924170426
43201CB00016B/2255